SELECTION AT THE TOP

AN ANNOTATED BIBLIOGRAPHY

SELECTION AT THE TOP

AN ANNOTATED BIBLIOGRAPHY

Valerie I. Sessa
Richard J. Campbell

Center for Creative Leadership
Greensboro, North Carolina

The Center for Creative Leadership is an international, nonprofit educational institution founded in 1970 to foster leadership and effective management for the good of society overall. As a part of this mission, it publishes books and reports that aim to contribute to a general process of inquiry and understanding in which ideas related to leadership are raised, exchanged, and evaluated. The ideas presented in its publications are those of the author or authors.

The Center thanks you for supporting its work through the purchase of this volume. If you have comments, suggestions, or questions about any Center publication, please contact Walter W. Tornow, Vice President, Research and Publication, at the address given below.

Center for Creative Leadership
Post Office Box 26300
Greensboro, North Carolina 27438-6300

CENTER FOR CREATIVE LEADERSHIP

CCL No. 333

Library of Congress Cataloging-in-Publication Data

Sessa, Valerie I.
    Selection at the top : an annotated bibliography / Valerie I. Sessa and Richard J. Campbell
        p. cm.
    ISBN 1-882197-29-1
    1. Executives—Selection and appointment—Bibliography. I. Campbell, Richard J. II. Title.
Z7164.C81S454 1997
[HF5549.5.S38]
016.6584'07112—dc21   97-8113
                                                                       CIP

General Contents

Complete Contents

Where They're From: Internal and External

Where They're From: Diversity

Other Issues

Transitions into the Position

Preface

The Center for Creative Leadership has had a long-standing interest in executive selection, beginning over a quarter of a century ago with our founder Smith Richardson, Sr. In 1992 that interest was reaffirmed in a conference held at CCL on executive selection, in which experts and others interested in the field shared their knowledge and ideas. With the conference as impetus, a new research effort on executive selection was initiated; it looks at issues around selection at the top three organizational levels (CEO and one and two levels down). The overall objective of the effort is to help improve the quality of leadership in organizations by discovering and disseminating information about executive selection.

To aid us in the development of the research, we began to identify and compile the important literature on executive selection. Numerous sources were consulted, such as scientific journals, technical reports, articles published in the popular press, books, and book chapters. The readings were initially summarized for our own purposes, but we soon realized that this information could also be useful to a much broader audience in the form of an annotated bibliography.

Such a bibliography would add to the body of knowledge referred to in four previous CCL reports: David DeVries' 1993 report, *Executive Selection: A Look at What We Know and What We Need to Know*, which extended what we already know about selection in the lower ranks of the organization up to selection in the upper ranks of management; George Hollenbeck's 1994 report, *CEO Selection: A Street-smart Review*, which summarized the writings of people we consider to be foremost authorities in CEO selection; Marian Ruderman and Patricia Ohlott's 1994 report, *The Realities of Management Promotion: An Investigation of Factors Influencing the Promotions of Managers in Three Major Companies*, which discussed how and why promotions occur in the executive suite; and Lorrina Eastman's 1995 bibliography on a related but distinctly separate topic, *Succession Planning: An Annotated Bibliography and Summary of Commonly Reported Organizational Practices*.

Our understanding of the selection literature, which is reflected in the more than 100 annotations in this bibliography, stands on the shoulders of this previous work, and we are grateful for the foundation. We are also grateful to CCL for making this report possible and particularly to Walt Tornow, vice president, research and publication, who suggested and supported it.

We thank CCL staff members, as well as colleagues outside of the organization, who helped make the project a reality. Peggy Cartner and Carol Keck of CCL's library staff helped us identify and obtain references on executives and executive selection that were used in this bibliography as well as for some of our other projects. Cheryl Schustack, a doctoral student at New York University, combed through numerous book report sections in academic journals for additional references.

Several CCL researchers and trainers were instrumental in helping us select and evaluate references and in finalizing the report. Bob Bailey, Marian Ruderman, and Jodi Taylor made suggestions to the final draft of the report, and Patricia Ohlott and Kathleen Holmes-Ponder contributed valuable feedback in their roles as internal reviewers. In addition, Mel Sorcher of Sorcher and Associates contributed considerable time and expertise as an external reviewer.

Many thanks to Joanne Ferguson, Marcia Horowitz, and Martin Wilcox for their editorial assistance and to Laurie Merritt for her administrative support.

Introduction

In this era of rapidly changing organizational environments, the task of executive selection is critical. Stories about CEO and top-management turnover can be found almost daily in the popular press. Those who study executive selection have estimated failure rates as high as 75% (Hogan, Raskin, & Fazzini, 1990); even the lowest estimates are put at 27% (Sessa & Campbell, 1997).

Practitioners clearly need help with such essential questions as: What does it mean to be successful in today's organizations? How can we select executives who are more likely to perform successfully in them?

The purpose of this report is to address these questions by providing an introduction to what recent literature says about selection at the top of organizations (CEO and one and two levels down) and how it relates to the selected executive's success and to the organization's goals.

The more than 100 annotations here reflect readings from a wide variety of sources, identified through *PsychLit* and *ABI Inform* databases and from recommendations from colleagues. They include scientific journal articles, technical reports, articles from the popular press, books, book chapters, and viewpoints of practitioners and experts in the field. The descriptions include information about executive selection at the CEO level (often labeled "succession") and two levels below, in large organizations as well as small, for-profit and not-for-profit organizations, in the U.S. as well as Europe.

Our rules for inclusion were that the sources had to be relatively current or considered classics (that is, they were cited often in the subsequent literature). All of the books and articles were published between 1983 and 1996. Additionally, the sources, in our estimation, had to have good ideas or impart important information. We also looked for scientific rigor in the articles published in scientific journals.

The contents of each annotation vary by source. In general, when writing each we included the reading's objective and then a summary of its contents. If the source reported research, we included a full description of the study including hypotheses, procedures, and findings.

To help make sense of the information, the annotations were categorized into seven chapters. The first contains descriptions of a broad overview of works that discuss the executive-selection process as a whole. The next six chapters organize the annotations to reflect the key areas in our research on executive selection.

These chapters are meant to address questions that may occur throughout a process of considering executive-selection initiatives; they focus on the individual executive, the organization, and on practical measures for developing executive-selection programs. Thus, the annotations in this report are organized to provide information about:

- *Overview of Selection at the Top.* A comprehensive look at the entire executive-selection process.
- *The Effect of Organizational Context.* The current and near-future business context and how it influences selection.
- *Characteristics of Jobs at the Top.* The characteristics of executive jobs at senior levels and what needs to be considered for an effective fit into a top-management team.
- *Characteristics of Executives.* What executives "look like" regarding demographics, personality, and leadership ability; also, information on the sources and pools of candidates according to whether they are internal or external and in terms of their demographic diversity.
- *Doing Selection and Prediction.* The actual selection process itself: "how-to," methods and predictors, and other issues that arise during selection and performance.
- *Executive Performance After Selection.* What happens once the executive is on the job in terms of transition into the position, success or failure, and transition out of the position.
- *Organizational Outcomes.* How executives and teams of executives matter to the goals of the organization.

This report is principally for executives who participate in selection procedures within their own companies, or who serve on boards of directors and thus select high-level executives in other companies. However, human resources managers, consultants, and members of executive-search firms, as well as organizational researchers, should also find the review of the literature helpful.

References

Hogan, R., Raskin, R., & Fazzini, D. (1990). The dark side of charisma. In K. E. Clark & M. B. Clark (Eds.), *Measures of leadership* (pp. 343-354). West Orange, NJ: Leadership Library of America, Inc.

Sessa, V. I., & Campbell, R. J. (1997). *Executive selection.* Paper presented at the 28th annual meeting of the Employment Management Association, Washington, DC.

How to Use This Report

Readers may approach this report in a variety of ways. Those new to the area of executive selection may want to read it in its entirety, starting with the synopsis at the beginning of each chapter. The synopsis contains highlights of the annotations, how the information in the annotated readings relates to selection, and what further information is needed for a more complete understanding of the issues covered in the section.

For those more familiar with executive selection, or who are interested in a particular aspect of it, the report is designed so that the reader can quickly go to specific areas of interest. For example, if information is sought on what measures organizations have taken to implement selection plans, one can turn directly to the chapter "Doing Selection and Prediction."

Within each chapter and section, annotations are in alphabetical order by the first author's last name. In the "Complete Contents," titles are listed alphabetically by author under the appropriate chapter and section heading. At the end of the book, the "Author Index" is an additional useful way to access the material.

OVERVIEW OF SELECTION AT THE TOP

The books and articles annotated here give a broad overview of selection at the top of organizations for those interested in taking a comprehensive look at the entire executive-selection process. Finkelstein and Hambrick (1996) incorporate selection under the broader topic of strategic decision-making at the top and describe a model including context, the selection itself, the selectee, and organizational consequences. Forbes and Piercy (1991) analyze indicators of CEO candidates over the course of their careers, beginning with entry into the organization. Brady and Helmich (1984) and Vancil (1987) look at successions directly into the CEO position, with Brady and Helmich approaching it from the organization point of view and Vancil approaching it from the CEO point of view. DeVries (1993) and Hollenbeck (1994) provide reviews of the literature. DeVries applies much of what we know about selections at lower levels to executive selection, and Hollenbeck reviews what the management experts are saying about CEO selection. Hogan, Curphy, and Hogan (1994) discuss the disconnect between what we know about selection at the top and how we use that knowledge.

What do these readings have to say about a successful executive-selection process? They take a broad look at executive selection from a variety of perspectives. Among them, there is general agreement (with the exception of Vancil) that current executive-selection processes are flawed. The authors generally concur that selectors at the top are novices at selection, they are not using the considerable body of information on how to select, and they may be limiting the number and range of potential candidates. Additionally, there is a general assumption among both practitioners and researchers that selection to top jobs is a wholly unique process (with each selection being different), and thus there is little research or theory specifically focused in this area. This suggests that before actually beginning the selection process, those involved may want to take a look at themselves and ask the following questions: What is the typical selection process in the company and is it generally successful or unsuccessful? What mechanisms are in place to get the team prepared for making a selection? Are all possible candidates under consideration?

What further information is needed to help with successful selection? To date, there is little descriptive information regarding the details of the entire process of how executives actually select other executives. The annotations in this chapter raise the following questions regarding this: Who are the decision-makers? What information do they collect about the organization, the job, and the candidates, and how do they collect it? What are the deciding factors for making a selection? How do they evaluate a selection? What role does organization context play? What differentiates a successful selection from an unsuccessful one?

Brady, G. F., & Helmich, D. L. (1984). *Executive succession: Toward excellence in corporate leadership.* Englewood Cliffs, NJ: Prentice Hall, Inc., 260 pages.

This book integrates research (much of it conducted by the two authors) and examples to describe succession at the top of organizations. Succession is defined as the movement of individuals through the role in an organization that is formalized as the most powerful of the power centers, controlling and directing the efforts of the organization toward its goals. Concentrating on executive succession to the CEO position from the organizational point of view (as opposed to either the executive team or the individual points of view), the authors enumerate the various ways that succession events occur and their antecedents and consequences.

Succession events include: outsider versus insider, length of CEO tenure, leadership style (task- or relationship-oriented), and successor needs. Antecedents include amount and type of organizational change. Consequences include turnover in the top-management team and organizational effectiveness measures.

Some of the major findings are: (1) The ratio of outside to inside CEOs is increasing. (2) Outsiders encounter different problems from insiders when assuming their role, including interpersonal problems, overcoming opposition from the company, winning the acceptance of insiders, and a general lack of knowledge about their job. (3) Outside successions are associated with greater turnover than inside successions. (4) Research does not support the notion that outsiders are higher achievers than insiders. (5) Demographics and context influence leadership styles. For example, outsiders, females, younger CEOs, and CEOs with short tenures are more likely to be task-oriented.

DeVries, D. L. (1993). *Executive selection: A look at what we know and what we need to know* (Rep. No. 321). Greensboro, NC: Center for Creative Leadership, 57 pages.

Through reviewing the published literature and participating in an executive-selection conference, DeVries provides the following nine observations: (1) After thirty years of research on personnel selection, we have learned much that could help increase the odds of picking successful executives (assuming that CEO and top-executive jobs are not unique). (2) Corporate executives are not using personnel selection tools. (3) Selection of executives will not be significantly improved until we learn to employ a holistic, context-rich look at the corporation, the job, and the candidates. (4) Selection of executives will not be significantly improved until both scholars and practitioners stop perpetuating the false distinction between selection and development. (5) Selection of executives will not be significantly improved until we stop measuring our success rate by using undifferentiated indicators of the person's success in making it up the corporate ladder. (6) While executive selection requires predicting how people will lead into the twenty-first century, we use models based on success in the 1970s. (7) Prior studies of executive selection have assumed that the candidates being reviewed are all internal to the organization. (8) We can learn much about executive selection by better understanding why it excludes women and people of color. (9) There is a sense of ennui among both behavioral scientists and practitioners about the work done to date in executive selection.

Finkelstein, S., & Hambrick, D. C. (1996). *Strategic leadership: Top executives and their effects on organizations*. New York: West Publishing Company, 457 pages.

Although this book is not strictly about executive selection, it is about decision making at the top of organizations, with the view that selection is one particular type of decision making. Using research, much of it their own, the authors discuss whether and how executives affect the bottom line, the psychological attributes of executives (values, cognitive models, and personality), executive experiences, and the importance of taking into account the top-management team. One chapter is devoted entirely to selection and turnover. (Other chapters include corporate governance and executive compensation.)

The authors present a model and propositions that explain why the previous top executive is departing (including performance, agency conditions, organizational characteristics, environment, and predecessor characteristics), and describes the succession event, successor characteristics (insider or outsider and similarity to the predecessor), and the effects of succession (organization and performance, stakeholder reactions). Finally, at the end of the book, the authors categorize contemporary research on strategic leadership. In their analysis of 146 works, they found 27 on succession (which is similar to selection). They conclude that stronger theory is needed in this area.

Forbes, J. B., & Piercy, J. E. (1991). *Corporate mobility and paths to the top: Studies for human resource management development specialists*. New York: Quorum Books, 208 pages.

The conclusion of the authors, based on their own research as well as theory and research developed by others, is that the executive-selection process for top executives is flawed and the best selections are not being made. Only a small number of candidates are being considered early in their careers, often by using subjective and biased data.

The authors outline the signals used by other executives to indicate future executive success. They include credibility, visibility, and familiarity and trust. In the early years (entering the workforce through promotion to general manager or functional vice president), credibility and visibility—the most important factors—are enhanced by education, entrance through a prestigious training program, first assignment in a powerful department, successful early performance in a critical functional area, tenure with the firm, early promotion into the managerial ranks, movement through functional areas, cross-functional and international assignments, positive assessment-center evaluation, and assistant-to-a-senior-executive assignments. These early years emphasize early selection to the fast track and short-term performance. Those who might be late bloomers are excluded from the running at this point.

In the middle years (general management or functional vice president through appointment to CEO), important promotion signals include general signals of familiarity and trust (socioeconomic origins, geographical origins, and education) as well as other credibility signals (generalist or specialist, functional expertise, and mobility).

The authors suggest that better selection requires the following: (1) wider search for executive talent, especially inside the firm (don't rely on the select few on the fast track); (2) collection and utilization of more relevant measures of performance; and (3) basing promotion decisions on these performance measures. This new system will reward for performance and not social origin, formal education, gender, or a career history that includes all the "right" moves.

Hogan, R., Curphy, G. J., & Hogan, J. (1994). What we know about leader-
    ship: Effectiveness and personality. *American Psychologist, 49*(6),
    493-504.

The premise here is that although psychologists know a great deal about
leadership, people who make decisions about leaders seem to ignore their
accumulated wisdom. This article defines leadership and then answers eight
questions, using leadership theory and research. Leadership is defined as
persuading other people to set aside for a period of time their individual
concerns and to pursue a common goal that is important for the responsibilities and welfare of a group.

The questions and answers are: (1) Does leadership matter? The authors
conclude that leadership does matter, but suggest that in U.S. industry the
majority of managers are incompetent. (2) How are leaders chosen? The
authors speculate that leaders are chosen on the basis of likability and fit to
upper management, not on competence or using assessment tools provided by
psychologists. (3) How should leaders be evaluated? Leaders should be
evaluated in terms of team and organizational effectiveness. (4) Why do we
choose so many flawed leaders? This is because candidates are chosen not on
established principles of personnel selection but on which candidates seem
most "leader-like." (5) How do we forecast leadership? The authors suggest a
combination of cognitive ability, personality, simulation, role play, and multi-
rater assessment instruments and techniques. (6) Why do leaders fail? They
fail because they have an overriding personality defect or character flaw that
alienates their subordinates and prevents them from building a team. Leader
effectiveness requires both the presence of positive characteristics and the
absence of the "dark side." (7) How do leaders build teams? This question
isn't really answered, but the authors suggest that the key to leader effectiveness is one's ability to build a team, and that the leader's personality has
effects on team performance. (8) What about leadership in workforce 2000?
The authors list five trends: the need for improvement in the quality of
management; closer scrutiny of senior-manager performance; the need to
change management practices to take into account the move toward a service
economy and the diversification of the workforce; the need to learn more
about how to manage creative talent; and the importance of using personality
measures to predict leader effectiveness.

Hollenbeck, G. P. (1994). *CEO selection: A street-smart review* (Rep. No. 164). Greensboro, NC: Center for Creative Leadership, 72 pages.

Hollenbeck reviews eight selected books on CEO selection written by a range of experts and makes sixteen important observations drawn from them: (1) Each CEO succession is unique. (2) Each CEO job is unique. (3) The CEO selection process is different from the selection processes for lower-level positions. (4) The responsibility for selecting the CEO resides with the board of directors, but that does not mean that the board makes the selection. (5) CEO selection is done by novices. (6) The CEO does make a difference in the performance of the organization. (7) The CEO's top-management team matters, too. (8) CEOs vary widely in how much discretion for action they have. (9) CEOs arrive in their jobs with schemas and repertoires that together make up their paradigms. (10) The selection of a new CEO has widespread implications for the organization and its members. (11) CEO selection is a long-term process. (12) CEO selection is an extremely complex process of matching a person with an uncertain future. (13) The criteria for CEO success are multiple and dynamic. (14) The actual process that decides who the next CEO will be is largely subjective, reflective, and based on personal observations. (15) Outsiders may participate in the CEO-selection process, their roles depending on their credibility. (16) The broad outlines of the process of CEO selection are evident, but a clear definition of the process has eluded us.

In conclusion, Hollenbeck suggests that there is little research on CEO selection, and that there are many good reasons for that. However, he suggests that the field is wide open and the time is ripe to begin studying this important subject.

Vancil, R. F. (1987). *Passing the baton: Managing the process of CEO succession.* Boston: Harvard Business School Press, 318 pages.

Although Vancil believes that a "science" for the topic of CEO succession is not likely because each succession is different, the primary objective of this book is to describe processes of several CEO successions (the non-public activities that occur before the formal succession announcement) and to explain why these occurred. He intends this information to be a learning tool for CEOs. However, for the succession decision, there is no learning curve; most CEOs have never made that sort of decision, and they will only make it once.

Vancil interviewed forty-eight executives (incumbent CEOs, prior CEOs, outside directors, and candidates to become CEOs). The names of these executives as well as the companies they were from were reported in case studies throughout. The book outlines the succession tasks a CEO must manage during his or her tenure, including understanding the strategic mandate, developing a pool of candidates, and presiding over the selection of a likely successor.

Findings include that there were two major sorts of successions: (1) passing the baton to a single chosen successor—basically a nonevent; and (2) a horse race of several contenders, yielding one winner and several losers. Most CEOs stay in their jobs for ten years (plus or minus two), and 25% of the CEOs are outsiders (an executive who has been employed by the company for five years or less).

In contrast to Forbes and Piercy (1991; in this section), Vancil concludes that the process seems to be working fairly well in U.S. organizations.

THE EFFECT OF ORGANIZATIONAL CONTEXT

One factor often omitted in both the actual process of selection at the top and in the selection literature is an understanding of the impact of the organizational context. The following set of annotations can alert those involved in selection at the top to potential blind spots. The readings in this chapter describe what the current and near-future business context is, and test hypotheses regarding how context influences selection.

Gupta (1992), Mahler (1993), and Sayles (1993) describe how the current environment is changing from the mass production environment to one with greater competition, shareholder activism, flatter structures, and characterized by a high rate of change. Hambrick and colleagues (1989) describe the predicted business environment rising during the 1990s into the year 2000. Those that theorize or test hypotheses regarding how context influences selections explore such contexts as organizational profitability, growth, industry instability, strategy, performance, size, and process and degree of change (Datta & Guthrie, 1994; Guthrie & Olian, 1991; Lundberg, 1986).

What do these readings have to say about a successful executive-selection process? They say two important things: First, context does have an impact on selection at the top; second, organizational contexts are in the midst of turbulent change. Due to these actualities, the costs of making a selection mistake are increasing. This suggests that for a successful selection, the selectors may want to spend considerable time discussing the internal environment (for instance, strategy, climate, changes, strengths, and needs) and external environment (for instance, industry ranking, market, competition, regulatory environment, future trends, and political instabilities) of the company, both in the present as well as in the predicted future, and use the organizational analysis to aid in the selection of a top executive.

What further information about organizational context is needed to help with successful selection? These readings deal with the theoretical and intangible, not with the practical. Although we can deduce that the changing context plays a role in selection, whether it is implicit or explicit, there is limited help given on how to analyze the organization environment and distill this analysis into a mechanism to aid with the selection of executives.

Datta, D. K., & Guthrie, J. P. (1994). Executive succession: Organizational
    antecedents of CEO characteristics. *Strategic Management Journal, 15*,
    569-577.

The objective of this study was to provide evidence that antecedent
conditions of firms are associated with the selection of CEOs. Using 195
successions found in the *Business Week 1000* between 1980-1989, study
findings demonstrated that firms with reduced organizational profitability
(using average ROA [return on assets] in the three years prior to the succession event) and firms with rapid growth (using percentage change in total
company sales over the three years preceding the CEO succession) are more
likely to hire outsiders (CEOs having fewer than five years of organizational
tenure at the time of the succession). R&D-intensive firms are more likely to
hire CEOs with technical backgrounds and higher levels of education.

Gupta, A. (1992). Executive selection: A strategic perspective. *Human
    Resource Planning, 15*(1), 47-61.

This article starts with the premise that three factors—rising intensity of
product-market competition, greater shareholder activism, and flatter structures with larger spans of control—have increased the costs of errors in CEO
and general-manager selection. As a result, the author suggests that it is
necessary to be more objective in the selection of executive leaders and that
executive selection needs to be tailored to the specific needs of the organization. The article discusses how executive paradigms affect organizational
outcomes (for example, differences in executives' tendencies to be selective
in their interpretations of and choice of action plans to deal with the same
objective reality); identifies sources and constraints on executive power; and
analyzes the executive-selection implications of positional differences for
three types of CEO/general managers: the SBU (small business unit) general
manager, the foreign subsidiary president, and the corporate CEO.
    Gupta advocates that selection committees address three key questions:
(1) How intense are the environmental as well as intra-organizational constraints on the incoming executive's power? (2) In light of its emergent
strategy, what are the organization's future capability needs? (3) What is the
cognitive and behavioral paradigm of each potential candidate?

Guthrie, J. P., & Olian, J. D. (1991). Does context affect staffing decisions? The case of general managers. *Personnel Psychology, 44*, 263-292.

The basic thesis of this article is that environmental contingencies affect the selection and removal of top organizational administrators to better align the organization with its environment. The authors develop and test hypotheses that predict relationships between organizational contextual features (industry instability, strategy, performance, and size) and background characteristics of general managers selected to head business units (organizational familiarity, functional experience, and age). Data were collected on forty general-manager selection decisions. Industry instability was measured using Rasheed and Prescott's industry sample [Rasheed, A., & Prescott, J. E. (1987). *Dimensions of task environments: Revisited.* Paper presented at the 47th annual meeting of the Academy of Management, New Orleans, LA], as well as the respondent's own assessment of industry instability. Strategy was indicated by each respondent's assessment of whether the business unit had a strategy of cost leadership or differentiation. Performance was measured by asking respondents to estimate the focal business unit's performance (sales, market share, operating profits, and ROI). Size was assessed using number of employees and sales revenue. The following general-manager background data was collected from the human resources director: tenure in corporation; tenure in SBU; functional experience ("internal focus"—accounting, finance, and manufacturing; and "external focus"—marketing and product R&D); and age.

Results indicate that industry instability, organizational strategy, and organizational size were associated with general managers' tenure levels, and that organizational strategy was associated with age.

Hambrick, D. C., Fredrickson, J. W., Korn, L. B., & Ferry, R. M. (1989). *Reinventing the CEO.* New York: Columbia University, 91 pages.

The objective of this report was to ask top executives at leading companies around the world about the challenges of the future business arena and to provide a prescription for how today's organizations and managers can prepare for those challenges. A 150-item questionnaire was completed by over 1,500 CEOs and senior executives from twenty nations.

Results showed the following. In terms of the challenges of the future business arena, all respondents predict increasingly intense competition (domestic and foreign as well as within their industry and outside) and high rates of technological change. In the U.S., top executives have more faith in the stability of the country, but see significant threats from high levels of government regulation and shortages of qualified personnel. CEOs will need to be expert in strategy formulation, human resource management, marketing and sales, and negotiation and conflict resolution. In terms of characteristics, ethics was rated most highly, followed by creativity, enthusiasm, open-mindedness, intelligence, inspiration, energy, encouragement, ability to be analytical, loyalty, physical fitness, organization, risk-taking attributes, diplomacy, intuition, and the willingness to be collaborative.

Among several other background experiences that CEOs will need (for example, education, functional experience, and formal training), the following emerged as important: business experience in turnarounds, diverse experiences, mergers and acquisitions, foreign assignments, membership on boards, and a long tenure in their major industry.

In the U.S., the authors suggest that top executives are discounting the importance of an international outlook, multilingualism, and foreign assignments, which may lead to parochialism and inhibit opportunity.

Lundberg, C. C. (1986). *The dynamic organizational contexts of executive succession: Consideration and challenges* (Tech. Rep.). Center for Effective Organizations, University of Southern California. Los Angeles: University of Southern California, 30 pages.

This report addresses the organizational context before and during the succession. Lundberg reviews different contexts, discusses the roles executives play in these contexts, and presents implications for executive selection and development. Contexts are seen as varying along two dimensions: (1) the process of change (natural evolutionary versus planned), and (2) the degree of impact (change, which is a better fit with elements, versus transformation, which is a shift in the organization's basic character). Contexts are also seen as taking place either within or between organizational "life stages."

Next, the author addresses what executive behaviors are called for by these different contexts, with the idea that organizations should select or develop executives who possess change and/or transformation competencies. Finally, the author discusses various questions that need to be addressed in the selection process, including: Is the succession anticipated? Is it planned for? When in the change process should it take place (does the successor plan the change process or only "do" it)? What kind of successor needs to be selected?

Mahler, W. R. (1993). *Self destruction at GM, IBM, and Sears: What can we learn from them?* Wyckoff, NJ: WRM Inc. Publishers, 178 pages.

This book explores the context within which several corporate giants, such as Sears, IBM, and GM, self-destructed in the early 1990s. The objective is to determine what went wrong and give opinions on how to ensure that other companies do not follow suit. Mahler suggests that the failure of these corporate giants was due, in part, to the top management.

In the first part of the book, Mahler discusses why these companies failed. According to his analysis, in all three organizations the basic nature of the business changed significantly, but the top management either didn't recognize the changes or refused to accept that the changes had occurred. He outlines seven reasons for the executive myopia: The executives were not broad-based business managers, were unable or unwilling to put in place a viable change, were risk-averse, and were more concerned with finishing their "tour of duty" rather than sustaining the institution; there was a faulty structure; there was little process in place for anticipating the future; and the board didn't have the power to intervene until a crisis occurred during which time the only alternative was to remove the chairman or CEO.

In part two, Mahler identifies ten decisions critical to transitioning a company on a self-destructive path to a successful one. Addressing these decisions will help organizations make fundamental changes. In part three, he outlines basic actions needed to avoid self-destruction.

Sayles, L. R. (1993). *The working leader: The triumph of high performance over conventional management principles.* New York: The Free Press, 277 pages.

Using case studies, Sayles asserts that contemporary managers face everyday, persistent turbulence that is much different from managing mass production (the fixed, unvarying routines on which many traditional and yet widely employed management paradigms are based). Organizations are now contending with demands for more and quicker responsiveness to customers, market, product, and process changes. This is compounded by internal departments who must compete and cooperate at the same time. In addition, there are an increasing number of specialists, multinational organizations, matrix organizations, and joint ventures.

To effectively handle the turbulent environment, today's leader must understand and be capable of managing workflow relationships not only within departments or functions but also at the boundaries. To do this a leader must be skilled at managing upward, influencing peers without authority, delegation, making constant changes as opposed to relying on static answers, flexibility, and technical competence. And senior executives need to understand that corporate success depends on execution, implementation, and expertise, and less on strategic decisions.

CHARACTERISTICS OF JOBS AT THE TOP

This chapter has two sections: (1) one about executive job descriptions and, (2) due to the increasing reliance on teams at the top, a description of what needs to be taken into account for an effective fit into top-management teams.

The information here is for those who are at the point in the selection process where they are determining what the executive job entails. It is especially important for those who are struggling with the realization that hiring an executive for a position is no longer enough, that this job also includes being part of the top-management team. The sources address the CEO's major area of focus (Washburn, 1994), in large corporations (Bruce, 1986) and in small organizations (Bruce, 1992). They also address the top-executive jobs in more general terms (Kaplan, 1986; see also Luthans, Hodgetts, & Rosenkrantz, 1988, in the "Executive Performance After Selection" chapter), including the necessity for handling increasing amounts of scope and scale (Bentz, 1987).

The sources on top-management teams take a slightly different tack. Here topics include conditions under which an integrated top-management team is needed (Michel & Hambrick, 1992), the forces that drive top-management members toward or away from becoming teams (Hambrick, 1994), and how to design a top-management team (Ancona & Nadler, 1986; Hambrick, 1987).

What do these readings have to say about a successful executive-selection process? A successful selection is no longer just fitting the right person into the job; now organizations must both fit the right person to the job and to the team. This makes creating the position and team description very important. These readings provide generalities; it is up to each organization to provide the specifics and details. Although many who hire at the top of organizations argue that the person they ultimately hire defines the position, it is still necessary to define the scope and scale of the position. It is also necessary to define what is to be performed in the position, as well as who the other team members are and their strengths, weaknesses, and working styles. Without this information, necessary knowledge, skills, abilities, and working styles may not become apparent until the executive brought into the position demonstrates a lack of them!

What further information is needed to help with successful selection? Sources such as these can only offer descriptions of executive positions in global terms—and they do just that. What is not addressed is how to go beyond the position description and determine what is needed in terms of the "soft side." The soft side refers to matters of fit, style, personality, and culture that are more interpersonal in nature than such things as scope and scale. For top-management teams, more research and theory is needed about helping CEOs and other top team members understand the conditions in which top-management teams are beneficial and when they are not, when to use teams, and how to design and select for the most effective teams for particular organizations and environmental conditions.

Executive Job Descriptions

Bentz, V. J. (1987). *Explorations of scope and scale: The critical determinant of high-level executive effectiveness* (Rep. No. 31). Greensboro, NC: Center for Creative Leadership, 37 pages.

Bentz defines the scope and scale of the executive-level position. Scope refers to the breadth of management, that is the number of units embraced within a position. Scale refers to the internal complexity, diversity, and ambiguity of functions within and across units managed, within and across varieties of personal relations, and across decisions made. The author then divides the report into three sections: measuring scope and scale, describing research supporting the construct, and outlining the experiences necessary for coping with scope and scale.

Scope and scale may be incrementally measured from low to high: responsibility for a single function; coordination of similar functions; coordination of multiple but related functions; integration and coordination of diverse functions within a single unit; integration and coordination of multiple diverse functions and units that are geographically dispersed; integration and coordination of two or more broad-based extended organizations, each marked by diversity of functions and geographic dispersion of units and responsible for company-wide integration and coordination of all units, functions, and territories.

To test the validity of scope and scale, Bentz used a criterion measure for job performance of 136 executives at high organizational levels to conduct a factor analysis; one of the nine factors that emerged centered on scope and scale.

Finally, he outlines the experiences essential for coping with scope and scale. These experiences were derived from secondary data sources and include: career preparation (supervisor in a local unit, staff experience in a local unit, manager of a small local unit, manager of a medium-sized local unit, staff position in the office of the general manager, manager of a large local unit, and assistant-to position); integration of experience; development of multidimensional thinking; and development of a cognitive map.

Bruce, J. S. (1986). *The intuitive pragmatists: Conversations with chief executive officers* (Rep. No. 310). Greensboro, NC: Center for Creative Leadership, 42 pages.

This report has two objectives: to determine how retired CEOs felt about their jobs and to determine what a CEO does. To accomplish these, Bruce interviewed thirteen retired CEOs of major U.S. companies. He describes the following components of the CEO job: gaining acceptance as the new CEO, creating relationships with senior management and the board of directors, maintaining other networks, learning to establish interfaces with the government, use of the media as a company figurehead, developing a relationship with predecessors, changing/maintaining strategic directions, and succession planning.

Bruce, J. S. (1992). *The creative opportunists: Conversations with the CEOs of small businesses* (Rep. No. 316). Greensboro, NC: Center for Creative Leadership, 51 pages.

In this report, Bruce interviews fourteen small-business owners and compares the information to his previous research on CEOs of large businesses (see next annotation). The interviews revealed a great deal about planning for succession in small businesses. From a combination of these interviews, Bruce categorizes five challenges for CEOs in any type of business: creating change, building a robust organization, dealing with employee concerns, building solid client/customer relationships, and providing resources.

CEOs of small businesses differ from CEOs of larger businesses in several ways: (1) They do not spend as much attention on planning a successor; they are busy designing the structure and parameter of the organization. (2) They often have family members as part of the top-management team. (3) They are often directly involved with their customers. (4) CEOs of small businesses make the rules as they go along, while CEOs of large companies usually must work within an already established rule structure.

Kaplan, R. E. (1986). *The warp and woof of the general manager's job* (Rep.
No. 27). Greensboro, NC: Center for Creative Leadership, 34 pages.

Kaplan and his colleagues conducted eleven interviews with general
managers to determine what they need to be able to do across all GM jobs, as
well as suggest where requirements might vary across situations. The GM
position is the first point at which several functions of the organization come
together; it is the lowest level of the executive echelon.

The interviews were content-analyzed into six important constants
about the jobs of GMs: ability to work with long-term direction and the big
picture; day-to-day activities; thinking multidimensionally as well as being
able to break down problems into parts; developing and maintaining large
networks; managing increases in scope (see reference by Bentz in this section); and handling the potentials and pitfalls of high position.

Certain characteristics of the job influence the extent to which the
above requirements are accomplished, including the business, the lines of
authority and structure, the priorities of the GM's superior, and the GM
himself or herself.

Washburn, S. A. (1994, March). Job description: Chief executive officer. *The
Corporate Board, 3*, p. 3.

Washburn defines the goals and objectives of the CEO along financial
lines (to optimize growth, profitability, and the value of shareholder equity)
and legal lines (to manage in accordance with the law, corporate bylaws and
policies, and procedures established by the board). He also defines the duties
and responsibilities of the position, discusses the authority invested in the
position, and suggests that the CEO is accountable to the board of directors.

Fitting into Top-management Teams

Ancona, D. G., & Nadler, D. A. (1986, September). Top hats and executive
tales: Designing the senior team. *Sloan Management Review*, pp. 19-28.

In response to the current trend of teams at the top of organizations,
Ancona and Nadler make the following six points. (1) They define an execu-

tive team as a group of people collectively providing strategic, operational, and institutional leadership. (2) Organizations are contending with greater external demands, organizational complexity, and succession. Team-based designs have emerged to increase coordination across functions and activities. (3) Executive teams are different from other teams because of the salience of the external environment, the complexity of the task, intensified political behavior, "fixed pie" rewards, increased visibility, composition, the special meaning or status of team membership, and the unique role of the CEO as the team leader. (4) Effectiveness can be measured in two dimensions: production of results and maintenance of effectiveness (teams' ability to satisfy members' needs, members' ability to work together over time, and teams' ability to adapt). (5) Teamwork needs to respond to different situations: complexity or instability of the external environment (high, low) and the degree of interdependence between major organizational units (high, low). (6) The authors discuss common problems in executive teams: synthetic teamwork, cosmetic teamwork, underdesigned teams, consensus management, "good plow/wrong field," inertia, and succession overhang.

Hambrick, D. C. (1987, September). The top-management team: Key to strategic success. *California Management Review*, pp. 88-108.

This article argues that the strategic success of a business depends not just on one person but on the entire top-management team. Hambrick proposes a framework for assessing and reshaping the top-management team. The framework includes: (1) assessing the context (for example, cultural and societal factors, business and industry environment, mission of the firm, strategic thrusts, key points of interdependence in the organization, human resource profile, and the capabilities or repertoire of the management team); (2) identifying the ideal team profile (for example, values, aptitudes, skills, knowledge, cognitive style, and demeanor); (3) assessing the existing team; (4) narrowing the gaps through replacements to the team, additions to the team, or development of current team members; and (5) looping back to the context—if the needed changes are not feasible, then the context must be changed.

Hambrick, D. C. (1994). Top management groups: A conceptual integration
    and reconsideration of the "team" label. *Research in Organizational
    Behavior, 16,* 171-213.

The objectives of this paper are twofold. The first is to develop a
framework for organizing theory and research on top-management groups on
the premise that the literature on this topic has grown profusely but in a
piecemeal and disjointed fashion. The framework delineates the parts of the
top-management group in terms of its composition, processes, incentives,
structure, and the group leader. The second objective is to discuss the tendency for top-management "groups" to cease being "teams." Hambrick
develops the centrifugal and centripetal forces that drive the groups toward or
away from behavioral integration (the degree to which the group engages in
mutual and collective interaction). These include size of the organization
(larger organizations have less integration); domain breadth (broader organizations have less integration); business strategy (using Miles and Snow's
typology [Miles, R. E., & Snow, C. C. (1978). *Organizational strategy,
structure, and process.* New York: McGraw-Hill], defender organizations
will have less integration than prospector organizations); organizational slack
(under conditions of very low and very high slack, integration will be low);
and environmental dynamism (the more dynamic the environment, the more
likely integration will be high).

Michel, J. G., & Hambrick, D. C. (1992). Diversification posture and top
    management team characteristics. *Academy of Management Journal,
    35*(1), 9-37.

The premise of this study is that an organization's diversification
posture determines the degree of integration it needs across business units,
which in turn influences the ideal composition of its top-management team.
The more tightly related a firm's businesses, the greater the need for integration and coordination among them. This need for integration influences the
composition of the top-management team, particularly in terms of cohesion
(tenure), corporate-wide operating knowledge base, and core functional
expertise. Archival data from 134 organizations revealed that in highly
integrated firms, top-management team members have longer tenures, less
tenure homogeneity, and more core-function expertise than top managers of
less integrated firms. Additionally, contrary to hypotheses, core-function

expertise is positively related to profitability for less integrated firms, whereas a strong negative relationship between performance and core-function expertise exists in highly integrated firms.

CHARACTERISTICS OF EXECUTIVES

This chapter includes annotations of readings in three areas: (1) who the top executives are as defined by individual differences, type, and leadership; (2) sources and pools of top executives in terms of internal and external candidates; and (3) sources and pools of top executives who are diverse.

These readings represent a mixture of topics as opposed to a unified body of literature. Despite the difficulty this presents for the reader, those who are interested in understanding where candidates for jobs at the top of organizations come from will find this chapter a good starting place. Sources address how top executives are similar to and different from others according to their demographic background (Kurtz, Boone, & Fleenor, 1989), personality (Berman & Miner, 1985), and leadership ability (Miller & Hanson, 1991). Three reports describe women executives (Catalyst, 1996a, 1996b, 1996c).

The readings here also demonstrate that organizations are increasingly looking to the outside to hire top executives (Hager, 1991; Jordan, 1993), why this is occurring (Cannella & Lubatkin, 1993; Dalton & Kesner, 1985; Puffer & Weintrop, 1995; Schwartz & Menon, 1985), and what considerations to take in deciding whether to look for an internal candidate or an external candidate (Geber, 1989; Kerr & Jackofsky, 1989).

The authors theorize about and test hypotheses regarding why there are few women in top-management positions (Kanter, 1993; Ohlott, Ruderman, & McCauley, 1994; Powell, 1988; Powell & Butterfield, 1994; Tharenou, Latimer, & Conroy, 1994; Van Velsor & Hughes, 1990). One reading discusses making it in the white majority corporate world from the black manager's point of view (Dickens & Dickens, 1991); a second addresses the impact of diversity in the middle to upper levels of the organization on practices, processes, and performance (Thomas & Ely, 1996); and a third addresses how to deal with people from different demographic backgrounds (Blank & Slipp, 1994).

What do these readings have to say about a successful executive-selection process? They suggest that candidates are developed, considered, and selected for a variety of reasons—individual, political, and structural—the least of which being their leadership ability. Important lessons from the readings in this chapter are that when considering candidates, selectors may want to take ample time to ensure that all qualified candidates are represented in the pool and that there is careful discussion regarding why a candidate should or shouldn't make it into the pool. Selectors should ask: Are candidates being considered for their abilities and fit to the job, or are there other factors that have placed them under consideration?

What further information is needed to help with successful selection? This area needs more unified programs of research. For example, what other ways do top executives differ from those who do not reach the top? More importantly, why do they differ, and is this in some way connected to actual skill levels? Under what circumstances is it better to hire an external candidate and under what circumstances is it better to hire internally? What is meant by an internal candidate or an external candidate? Definitions of external executives range from executives working outside the organization to executives working outside the predecessor's immediate team. Finally, although there was theory and research on how women differ from men, only one reading addressed theories or studies regarding what black managers must do to succeed. And no readings addressed the whole range of potential candidates who differ from the typical corporate elite (middle-aged, middle-class, white male) and how to ensure that the best are in the candidate pool.

Who They Are

Berman, F. E., & Miner, J. B. (1985). Motivation to manage at the top executive level: A test of the hierarchic role-motivation theory. *Personnel Psychology, 38,* 377-391.

This article attempts to fill the gap in the scientific literature regarding personality characteristics of those who head large corporations. The hypotheses of the study were that those who reach the highest levels of large bureaucratized business firms will have higher levels of motivation to manage, as measured by the Miner Sentence Completion Scale (MSCS), than individuals who have only achieved lower levels; and the scores of top executives who have worked their way up the organization indicate higher motivation than scores of top executives who either founded the company or are related by blood or marriage to the founder.

The top-executive sample included 75 (out of a sample of 300), 59 of whom were CEOs or COOs, and 16 of whom were either executive vice presidents or group vice presidents. Of these, 49 were bureaucratic managers and 26 were entrepreneurs and family managers. All were male. The comparison sample included 65 lower- or mid-level managers who were rated as average or good and whose ages were within three years of the top executives. All but four were males. The executives filled out the MSCS which measures six managerial role prescriptions: authority figures, competitiveness (competitive games, competitive situations), assertive role, imposing wishes, standing out from the group, and routine administrative functions. Using t-tests, hypotheses were supported.

Catalyst. (1996a). *1996 Catalyst census of women board directors of the Fortune 500.* New York: Author, 32 pages.
Catalyst. (1996b). *1996 Catalyst census of women corporate officers and top earners.* New York: Author, 38 pages.

These two reports were developed with the idea that "what gets measured gets done." The first census found that women hold just over 10% of board seats, yet make up less than 1% of inside directors—83 Fortune 500 companies have no women on their board. The second census revealed that women account for 1,302 of a total of 13,013 corporate officers in Fortune

500 firms; 78% (394) of Fortune 500 firms have one or more women corporate officers.

Additionally, women account for 47 of a total of 2,500 top earners (1.9%). The 1,251 senior women executives contacted in the study in the following Catalyst report had an average compensation of $248,000 (median $218,000).

Catalyst. (1996c). *Women in corporate leadership: Progress and prospects.*
New York: Author, 91 pages.

This report addresses women's advancement from the perspective of women who have made it to senior levels of leadership in Fortune 1000 firms. The report's objective is to compare the perspectives of CEOs and women who have advanced to top levels in U.S. corporations on these subjects: career paths and experiences; impediments to advancement; and effective career-development practices and work/life balance strategies.

Data were collected from 461 women holding titles of vice president and above who work in Fortune 1000 companies (a response rate of 37%). In-depth telephone interviews were conducted with 20 of these women. Data were also collected from 325 CEOs (response rate of 33%), with 20 agreeing to further in-depth interviews.

One finding suggests that the personal strategies these women found important to their career success include: exceeding performance expectations, developing a style with which male managers are comfortable, seeking out difficult or challenging assignments, and having influential mentors.

The most important corporate strategies for advancing women include giving them visible assignments, developing high-potentials, providing cross-functional job rotation, and sending them to external executive-development programs.

Kurtz, D. L., Boone, L. E., & Fleenor, C. P. (1989). *CEO: Who gets to the top in America?* East Lansing: Michigan State University Press, 204 pages.

Using biodata and personal information on family background, social class, characteristics and habits, marriage, religion, education, early signs of a business career, leisure interests, and management style provided by over 200 CEOs, the authors paint a picture of the typical CEO in the United States. The majority of these CEOs have been married over fifteen years and have strong religious commitments. Typically, CEOs are middle class and come from two-parent families in the midwest. They are highly educated, tend to be organized and in good physical condition, are less likely to smoke, and engaged in a myriad of extracurricular activities (both sports and clubs) during school.

Miller, A. F., Jr., & Hanson, M. (1991, October). The smile on the face of the leadership tiger. *Personnel Management,* pp. 54-55.

This article suggests that many organizations seeking leaders for major responsibilities are confusing leadership with some of the behavioral characteristics that some leaders exhibit. Using their System for Identifying Motivated Abilities (SIMA) on four groups that included a total of 398 mid-level and executive managers, the authors found that they were influencers but not leaders. Influencers are able to influence others and get others to accept their ideas, are good communicators, want a combination of roles, and are willing to be involved in a team effort if they have a defined individual role. However, few were motivated and competent to manage others or exercise sustained leadership over others. Influencers are reluctant to confront others over poor performance; are not often motivated or able to make complex, risky decisions; are not proactive; and want to know clearly what they have to do to be successful. The authors conclude that most of the people running the organizations in the study are not leaders; they only look as though they are.

Where They're From: Internal and External

Cannella, A. A., Jr., & Lubatkin, M. (1993). Succession as a sociopolitical process: Internal impediments to outsider selection. *Academy of Management Journal, 36*(4), 763-793.

Traditional theory suggests that poor organizational performance will increase the likelihood that an outsider (any successor with less than two years of service in their firm) will be selected to succeed a firm's chief executive. In this study, the authors hypothesize that sociopolitical forces will moderate this performance-selection link; that is, poor performance will only lead to outsider selection when sociopolitical forces are weak.

Data from 1,187 succession events were drawn from the *Forbes* annual June issues on executive compensation (1971-1985). For inclusion in the sample, the successions also had to be mentioned in *The Wall Street Journal*. Daily market returns on the company could be retrieved from the Center for Research on Securities Prices tapes; and the formal title of CEO had to pass from one person to another, resulting in a final sample of 472 succession events.

Sociopolitical forces included the presence or absence of an heir-apparent and the incumbent's ability to influence the selection decision (the incumbent retains the chairperson title). Performance was measured by return on equity (ROE; adjusted by industry average); Capital Asset Pricing Model (CAPM); Jensen's alpha; and both systematic risk (market risk) and unsystematic risk (variance in shareholder returns that could not be explained by movements in the market). CEO turnover was defined as a relay succession, a normal retirement, an early retirement, death or poor health, or a dismissal (all officership and directorship connections severed). Evidence using logistic regression analyses support hypotheses.

Dalton, D. R., & Kesner, I. F. (1985). Organizational performance as an antecedent of inside/outside chief executive succession: An empirical assessment. *Academy of Management Journal, 28*(4), 749-762.

The authors hypothesized that the choice of an outside CEO (one who is not in the predecessor's span) will be associated with poor organizational performance in the period prior to succession. Performance was measured using both investor returns (end-of-the-month closing stock prices for the three years prior to succession) and accounting returns (average return on equity for the same period).

Using companies on the New York Stock Exchange reported to have experienced an executive succession in a one-year period (*n*=96), they found little support for their hypothesis. Instead, only those companies with mid-range performance (using both investor and accounting indicators) chose outside successors. By contrast, neither poorly performing nor highly performing companies did.

Geber, B. (1989, February). Should you build top executives . . . or buy them? *Training*, pp. 25-32.

This article discusses the pros and cons of hiring insiders and outsiders. Insiders may be good because they are known quantities, assuming the company is doing a good job of developing from within. Outsiders may be good because they are "fresh blood," or there are pressing needs for someone with skills no one in the organization has. On the downside, outsiders may suffer from "tissue rejection" because they don't know the business, the culture, or the company's informal networks. Additionally, disgruntled insiders who were passed over may either leave the organization or stage an underground resistance.

Hager, B. (1991, August 12). CEO wanted. No insiders, please. *Business Week*, pp. 44-45.

This article argues that more and more companies are turning to outsiders for jobs at the top. According to E. Jennings (professor emeritus at Michigan State University's Eli School of Management), 28% of all newly hired CEOs at 385 companies were outsiders in 1991.

Jordan, M. (1993, October 11). CEOs with the outside edge. *Business Week*, pp. 60-62.

Quoting Professor Emeritus E. Jennings from Michigan State University, this article suggests that the number of CEOs selected from the outside is rising. In the first part of 1993, 35% of the fifty-one new CEOs were outsiders.

Kerr, J., & Jackofsky, E. (1989). Aligning managers with strategies: Management development versus selection. *Strategic Management Journal, 10*, 157-170.

This article discusses the difference between achieving alignment between managers and strategies through development and through selection.

The authors suggest that more effective organizations will exhibit congruence between their strategy (for example, steady state versus evolutionary), level of integration, and culture (for example, clan versus market culture), and their alignment strategies (development versus selection). Companies that tend toward a steady state, high integration, and clan culture would be more effective if they used a development model; while companies that tend toward an evolutionary, low integration, and market culture would be more effective if they used a selection model.

Puffer, S. M., & Weintrop, J. B. (1995). CEO and board leadership: The influence of organizational performance, board composition, and retirement on CEO successor origin. *Leadership Quarterly, 6*, 49-68.

This study investigated the impact of three variables on the decision to appoint an internal or external successor to the CEO: corporate performance, the proportion of insiders to outsiders on the board of directors, and the reason for succession (result of retirement versus all others). The sample consisted of 240 firms whose CEOs had been appointed between 1978 and 1984, using the annual *Forbes* magazine surveys of the 800 highest paid executives. Additionally the firm had to be traded on the New York or American Stock Exchange and have financial data reported on the CRSP and COMPUSTAT.

Outsiders were measured three different ways: having one year or less organizational tenure, having three years or less tenure, and having five years or less tenure. Corporate performance was measured using cumulative abnormal security (CAS) returns of the firm for the year prior to the change in CEO. CAS represents the actual return minus the normal or predicted return. CEOs who were sixty-four or older when they left were defined as retirements. Those who were less than sixty-four were seen as leaving for reasons other than retirement.

Analyses using moderated logistic regression analyses demonstrated that poor organizational performance and a greater proportion of outside members on the board of directors were associated with the tendency to appoint external successors when the previous CEO was below retirement age, but not when the previous CEO had reached traditional retirement age.

Schwartz, K. B., & Menon, K. (1985). Executive succession in failing firms. *Academy of Management Journal, 28*(3), 680-686.

The authors hypothesized that failing firms would be more likely to change CEOs in the three years preceding their filing for bankruptcy. They further tested for the effect of firm size on CEO replacement and the relative likelihood of insider and outside succession in failing firms. Insider successions are from within the organization. External successions are those where the CEO is brought in directly from the outside (these definitions are different from the Brady and Helmich book in the "Overview of Selection at the Top" chapter; and the Dalton and Kesner article, this section). Organization size was measured using the operating sales revenue. Failing firms were companies that had filed for bankruptcy petitions during the years 1974 to 1982 and traded on the New York or American Stock Exchange (*n*=134).

These were matched by companies with similar industry and size (revenue dollars) four years prior to the failing firm's bankruptcy. Financial distress was associated with the tendency to change CEOs; and the closer the companies got to filing for bankruptcy, the more likely they were to change CEOs. The results also showed that failing firms were more likely to go outside than were solvent firms. Finally, the relatively larger failing firms displayed a stronger preference for external successions than the smaller failing companies. Size did not have a similar influence on the control sample.

Where They're From: Diversity

Blank, R., & Slipp, S. (1994). *Voices of diversity: Real people talk about problems and solutions in a workplace where everyone is not alike.* New York: AMACOM, 212 pages.

This how-to book is written from the perspectives of people from different demographic backgrounds, including African Americans, Asian Americans, Latinos, recent immigrants, workers with disabilities, younger and older workers, gays and lesbians, women, and white men. The book works from the premise that many people are uncomfortable dealing with people who are not like themselves and don't realize when they are being insensitive to others.

Using the words of the members of each group, the authors point out categories of what offends them and what they resent about their treatment in the workplace. After describing the perspectives of each group, the authors present workplace examples and suggestions on what managers should say and how they should act.

Dickens, F., & Dickens, J. B. (1991). *The black manager: Making it in the corporate world* (Rev. ed.). New York: AMACOM, 446 pages.

This work, first written in 1982 and updated in 1991, represents theory, research, and applied learnings regarding the attitudes, emotions, behaviors, and job skills learned by black managers in adjusting to and becoming successful in the white corporate world. Here, success is defined as earning at least one promotion in the company.

Through interviews with black managers (little else was said about the research), the authors develop a four-phase developmental model including entry, adjusting, planned growth, and success. For each phase, attitudes, emotions, behaviors, and job skills are examined in depth, using a case study to exemplify the stage. After describing each stage, the authors outline solutions and basic concepts to situations encountered by black managers in each phase.

Kanter, R. M. (1993). *Men and women of the corporation* (Updated ed.). New York: Basic Books, 390 pages.

This seminal work, first written in 1977 and updated in 1993, outlines Kanter's theory regarding why men and women hold different roles in the organization. Using a structural model, Kanter proposes that it is not an individual-level problem (which suggests that men and women must change) but that responses to work are a function of basic structural issues, such as the constraints imposed by roles and the effects of opportunity, power, and numbers (which suggests that it is the organization that must change).

Kanter has five assumptions underlying her model: (1) Work is not an isolated relationship between actor and activity, but must include the setting. (2) Behavior in organizations is adaptive. (3) If behavior reflects a "reasonable" response to an organizational position, then the behavior is not inevitable. (4) Behavior is also directly connected to the formal tasks set forth in a job's location in the division of labor. (5) Interest in the relationship of formal task, formal location to behavioral responses also leads to an emphasis on competence.

Instead of comparing differences in men and women, Kanter compares differences along three components. The first component of her model, opportunity, addresses expectations and future prospects. Those who are low in opportunity differ from those high in opportunity in terms of aspirations for growth, self-esteem, commitment to and satisfaction with the organization, comparison groups (horizontal instead of upward), and so forth. Power, or the capacity to mobilize resources, includes the discretion imbedded in the job, visibility, relevance, and status. Those who are low in power differ from those high in power in terms of morale, leadership behaviors, status, and so forth. Proportion is the relative amount of a particular group or type. Those who are represented in a very small proportion differ from those in a very high proportion by being more visible and "on display" as opposed to fitting in; they try to become socially "invisible," have a hard time gaining credibility, feel more pressure to conform, feel more isolated, and so forth. In her update, Kanter believes that the variables that determined success in the 1970s are still relevant in the 1990s.

Ohlott, P. J., Ruderman, M. N., & McCauley, C. D. (1994). Gender differences in managers' developmental job experiences. *Academy of Management Journal, 37*(1), 46-47.

The authors propose and test two hypotheses that men and women experience different developmental opportunities in their jobs. Hypothesis one is that men experience more job transitions and task-related job components than women; hypothesis two is that women experience greater obstacles than men. They collected data using an instrument, the *Developmental Challenge Profile®: Learning from Job Experiences,* on 281 men and 226 women (73% response rate), from five corporations and one government organization. The respondents were managers through the level of vice president.

In terms of hypothesis one, results suggest that men do perceive receiving more task-related developmental activities such as higher stakes, managing business diversity, and handling external pressure; but do not differ on developing new directions, inherited problems, reduction decisions, problems with employees, job overload, or the job transition scale of unfamiliar responsibilities. Women scored higher than men on one task-related scale: influencing without authority. For hypothesis two, results suggest that women are higher on only one obstacle scale: lack of personal support.

Powell, G. N. (1988). *Women and men in management.* Newbury Park, CA: Sage Publications, 260 pages.

The purpose of this book is to help men and women in both managerial and nonmanagerial roles to understand others' needs, attitudes, skills, and goals. Using his own and others' research, Powell explores traditional views of women and men; sex (biological) and gender (societal) differences; and men and women in organizations, including career paths, stereotypes, and equal employment laws.

He finds that "traditional" beliefs about women are not really traditional at all (although beliefs for men are more so); that although there are large differences in early occupational aspirations and expectations, smaller sex differences exist in decisions to work, and even smaller sex differences exist in decisions about job opportunities; and that for the most part men and women managers do not differ.

Further, Powell says that barriers for women into male-dominated occupations are breaking down, but balanced sex ratios are seldom achieved. Also, there are differences in men's and women's general career patterns—women with families are less likely to pursue careers in management than men with families, more male managers have stay-at-home spouses than female managers, and the woman continues to perform most household chores—though these differences appear to be diminishing. Although almost all work organizations have acted to provide more equal opportunities to their employees and applicants, these are often token attempts. Finally, sexual harassment is defined. The author claims that what should be done about it is seen differently by men and women and that it still occurs at an alarming rate.

Powell, G. N., & Butterfield, D. A. (1994). Investigating the "glass ceiling" phenomenon: An empirical study of actual promotions to top management. *Academy of Management Journal, 37*(1), 68-86.

This study examined promotion decisions for U.S. federal government senior-executive service positions in a cabinet-level department. Hypotheses concerned both direct and indirect effects of gender, such that women would receive less favorable decision outcomes than men. "Less favorable" was measured in three ways: (1) the review panel's evaluation; (2) referred for the position (made the first cut); and (3) selected for the position. Data were collected using review panels and applications for 438 people applying for thirty-two positions.

Contrary to the hypotheses, the job-irrelevant variable of gender worked to women's advantage, both directly and indirectly.

Tharenou, P., Latimer, S., & Conroy, D. (1994). How do you make it to the top? An examination of influences on women's and men's managerial advancement. *Academy of Management Journal, 37*(4), 899-931.

Researchers tested three models of career advancement (overall, women's, men's) using confirmatory factor analysis. The models included organizational structure (male hierarchy), career encouragement, training, home status (spouses, number of children), amount of work experience, parental education encouragement, self-confidence, education, and managerial advancement (position on hierarchy, salary, number of subordinates). Data were gathered from 513 women and 501 men managers on six managerial levels in public and private Australian organizations.

Although analyses demonstrated that the overall model fit the data, the authors tested and found differences by sex. For women, educational encouragement had a positive influence on education, which had a positive impact on advancement. Self-confidence had an impact on career encouragement and training and development; career encouragement also had an impact on training and development, which had a positive impact on advancement. Home status had a negative impact on work experience; work experience had a positive impact on training and development. Age was also related to both work experience and advancement.

Slight differences were found for the male model. Work experience and education influence men's training more positively. Training then has a more positive impact on men's advancement. Home status had a positive influence on work experience, and unexpectedly organizational structure had a negative impact on training and development. Finally, age influenced work experience but not advancement.

Thomas, D. A., & Ely, R. J. (1996, September-October). Making differences matter: A new paradigm for managing diversity. *Harvard Business Review,* pp. 79-90.

This article outlines a small portion of the research that the authors have been conducting for the past six years. Their original research questions were: (1) How do organizations successfully achieve and sustain racial and gender diversity in their executive and middle-management ranks? (2) What is the impact of diversity on an organization's practices, processes, and performance? (3) How do leaders influence whether diversity becomes an enhancing or detracting element in the organization?

The authors collected data from twelve companies (through interviews, surveys, archives, and observations), which included a law firm, a community bank, a consulting firm, financial services firms, Fortune 500 manufacturing companies, high-tech companies, a private foundation, and a university medical center.

Results yielded three paradigms for managing diversity. The first two encompass traditional views of diversity and are called the *discrimination-and-fairness paradigm* and the *access-and-legitimacy paradigm.* These two paradigms may actually inhibit effectiveness. The third, the *learning-and-effectiveness paradigm,* goes beyond defining diversity as racial, national, gender, and class representation to realizing that diversity should be understood as the varied perspectives and approaches to work that members of different identity groups bring. Companies using the third paradigm incorporate employees' perspectives into the main work of the organization and enhance work by rethinking primary tasks, practices, markets, products, strategies, missions, and cultures.

Van Velsor, E., & Hughes, M. W. (1990). *Gender differences in the development of managers: How women managers learn from experience* (Rep. No. 145). Greensboro, NC: Center for Creative Leadership, 122 pages.

This study centered around the question, "Why are companies finding it so difficult to include women in executive ranks?" The authors used secondary data sources to create their sample of 189 men and 78 women. These individuals were from predominantly Fortune 100-sized firms, who had participated in studies designed to determine key events that had taken place in their careers and what they learned from them.

Although both men and women report many similar experiences and learnings, men additionally report experiences with lessons that deal with learning new skills and how to be accountable. Women, on the other hand, report experiences with lessons that deal primarily with focusing on the self/environment fit.

Why are there differences? Many of the assignments that men report the most learning from are those where women have little or no involvement. Additionally, women may learn different lessons from events similar to those discussed by men.

DOING SELECTION AND PREDICTION

There are three sections in this chapter: (1) "How-to" references, which outlines major issues and processes to consider when hiring top executives; (2) specific methods and predictors, which discusses actual tools and early career predictors used in hiring top executives; and (3) other issues during selection and appraisal, such as politics and human shortcomings of the selectors.

The reader will find information here about the heart of the selection process; it is what many people think of or want when they hear the words *executive selection*. The "how-to" readings discuss selection processes in a variety of settings, including not-for-profit organizations (Garrison, 1989) and the banking industry (Hallagan, 1991). These works approach the process from a number of viewpoints, including those of executives and managers (Gilmore, 1988; Pinsker, 1992; RHR International, 1991; Sorcher, 1985; Valentine, 1991; Van Clieaf, 1992), boards of directors (Hallagan, 1991; Kenny, 1994; McCanna & Comte, 1986; Ross, 1989), and search firms (Gerstein & Reisman, 1983). Two articles address problem areas in the selection process (Levinson, 1994; Pinsker, 1992).

Methods vary from simple biographical data (Russell, 1990), to the more complex assessment center (Howard, 1992), to a series of procedures (Baehr, 1992), to handwriting analysis (Shackleton & Newell, 1991). Predictors include human-capital variables, demographics, motivation, and job experiences (Howard & Bray, 1988; Judge, Cable, Boudreau, & Bretz, 1994, 1995; Lindsey, Homes, & McCall, 1987; McCall, Lombardo, & Morrison, 1988). Other issues that affect the selection process include politics (Gioia & Longnecker, 1994; Zald, 1965), cognitive and personality shortcomings (Hitt & Barr, 1989; Kets de Vries, 1988; Ruderman & Ohlott, 1990), and organizational factors (Ruderman & Ohlott, 1994).

What do these readings have to say about a successful executive-selection process? Selection typically is more than an antiseptic choosing of the right person for the job; it involves politics, human shortcomings, and situational factors. The readings demonstrate that there is no "magic bullet" when it comes to selection; there is no universal correct selection process, no universal predictive measure, and no universal correct selection method. In fact, selectors are not using the more sophisticated selection tools, they are not making selections based on sophisticated judgments, nor are they validating the procedures that they are using (Ryan & Sackett, 1987; Sackett, 1992; White & DeVries, 1990).

What does this say to executives who are trying to make a selection? Outline the process that works best for the company and the particular job. Involve multiple people in the decision-making process. Spend time analyzing the company's needs and the top requirements. Use multiple predictors and measures for getting information about the candidates. And finally, evaluate the selection process; ask if the executive was successful. If not, why not? What in the selection procedure could be changed to improve the probability of success?

What further information is needed to help with successful selection? Although there is information regarding how to do an executive selection, it was surprisingly difficult to find predictors and methods specifically targeting executives (although there is a plethora of information on selection at lower levels). Unfortunately, many of the "how-to" readings do not back their suggested processes with research demonstrating the effectiveness of such processes. As to methods and predictors, discussion centers on getting information, but little time is spent discussing what information to attain from candidates—that is, what is the best method for getting different types of the information needed and how do selectors make the best decision once the information is gathered.

"How-to"

Garrison, S. A. (1989). *Institutional search: A practical guide to executive recruitment in nonprofit organizations.* New York: Praeger, 168 pages.

This book is aimed at a different population than many of the other books and articles in this bibliography: that is, search committee members charged with hiring a new top executive in a not-for-profit institution. Not-for-profits are different from for-profit organizations in that they are usually started by a motivated person with a cause and are expected to endure for generations or even centuries. The organization structures, concept of time, concept of service, and the political process are also typically different. Due to the large number of nonprofits (838,000 institutions, approximately 6% of the GNP, and supporting 10% of the workforce), selection at the top is an important issue. Garrison estimates that a minimum of 10,000 to 15,000 searches take place each year at the top level and two levels down in not-for-profits such as schools, symphonies, operas, ballets, art museums, park boards, and so forth. The book covers all steps of the search process including forming a search committee, developing search specifications, where to find candidates, screening candidates, interviewing, and convincing those who say "no" to say "yes." It also covers some materials that we haven't found addressed in other areas, including a discussion of why confidentiality is important during the search and considering the family (and helping the spouse search for a job).

Gerstein, M., & Reisman, H. (1983). Strategic selection: Matching executives to business conditions. *Sloan Management Review, 24*(2), 33-49.

The purpose of this article is to outline the selection strategy used by Gerstein, Reisman, & Associates: that is, matching individuals to specific position requirements. Although this strategy is an assumption of selection for lower-level jobs, its application to executive jobs has been slow because of the following beliefs: (1) Management is considered mysterious and defies objective analysis; "style" and "fits in" are too abstract and too sensitive to identify and measure. (2) There is pressure to reward performance with promotion. (3) There is a stronger desire to match candidates with the selectors, not with the job requirements. (4) Executives are rarely trained in selection, but are expected to do it well. (5) There is a belief in the "universal manager."

Current practices are weak because the language used is vague and imprecise; job descriptions are given little time and effort; and executives only have access to the behaviors they observe firsthand. To correct for these problems, the authors use the following process: (1) specification of business condition and strategic direction; (2) confirmation or modification of organization structure; (3) development of role descriptions for each key job in the structure; (4) assessment of key personnel; (5) matching individuals with positions; and (6) implementation. The assessment techniques used include behavioral interviewing and assessment center testing.

Gilmore, T. N. (1988). *Making a leadership change: How organizations and leaders can handle leadership transitions successfully*. San Francisco: Jossey-Bass, 279 pages.

This book, written for executives and managers, has three underlying premises: (1) Leadership does make a critical difference. (2) Leadership transitions are particularly significant moments in an organization's history. (3) These high-leverage opportunities are often not used with executives; instead, decision-makers rely on luck rather than intelligent strategies for success.

Divided into four sections, in Part One, Gilmore examines the increasing importance of leadership and the recent acceleration in leadership turnover. Part Two addresses the stages in an active leadership search. Here he defines eight stages in a leadership transition: (1) a decision to seek a change in leadership; (2) the design of a search-and-selection process; (3) an analysis of the strategic challenges facing the organization; (4) the translation of the strategic assessment into specific leadership needs and job qualifications; (5) a search for prospective candidates; (6) the screening and initial selection of finalists; (7) the interviewing and final selection of candidates; and (8) the transition process.

In Parts Three and Four, Gilmore addresses in depth the area often ignored in the selection literature: managing the critical transition period as the new leader begins to take charge in terms of process and the major issues (including setting a new direction, reorganizing, building alliances, and managing change).

Hallagan, R. E. (1991). Picking the proper CEO. *Bottomline, 8*(5), 25-27.

Hallagan argues that when there is an opening for a new CEO, the board of directors should take the opportunity to step back and reassess the firm (in this case it is the banking industry) and the CEO role. The following steps are suggested: (1) Reassess the bank's vision, analyze its strengths and weaknesses, and project where you want the bank positioned in three-to-five years. (2) Identify the most difficult tasks required of the new CEO, identify critical success factors, and decide how to measure the success or failure of the new CEO. (3) Decide what skills, character traits, management style, chemistry/fit issues, and type of track record or accomplishments are required. (4) Target positions and companies (Where would the ideal candidate be now?). (5) Do a reality check; are these things realistic? (6) Review internal candidates. (7) Review outside candidates using the target list and ideal profile.

Kenny, R. M. (1994, March). The board's stake in succession planning. *The Corporate Board*, pp. 1-2.

Kenny suggests that boards of directors need to take a more active role in the succession process for CEOs. The board should get involved early in the succession process, they should take the lead (over the CEO) in choosing the successor, and the former CEO should leave the board when he or she retires from the company.

Levinson, H. (1994). Beyond the selection failures. *Consulting Psychology Journal, 46*, 3-8.

Levinson suggests that the failure of many of the top executives in the early 1990s was due to errors in selection. These errors were due to the inadequacy of search firms because of their lack of psychological-assessment skills and the limits of the psychological methods used (they are cross-sectional, they are often "canned" printouts of ready-made interpretations, and the correlations between tests and criteria are inadequate).

To do an accurate assessment, the selection should take into account three elements: the psychology of the individual, the psychology of the boss and the boss's boss, and the nature of the organization. Only then can a psychologist adequately evaluate the degree of fit between the candidate and the job.

McCanna, W. F., & Comte, T. E. (1986, May). The CEO succession dilemma: How boards function in turnover at the top. *Business Horizons*, pp. 17-22.

The authors question the assumption that succession is an attempt to find the person to implement a particular strategy rather than to formulate one. It is not always the case that a strategy is in place. Should the board formulate the strategy before hiring a new CEO or hire a new CEO to formulate and implement the strategy? Can the board formulate a strategy? The authors conclude that no board can develop a strategy that reflects the best the firm has to offer. Therefore the board must choose someone to both create and implement the strategy. This person should come from within the industry and have a thorough knowledge of the technology and the practices of the industry.

Pinsker, R. J. (1992, May). The seven deadly sins in hiring executives, managers, and professionals. *Manage*, pp. 32-34.

The author outlines seven mistakes commonly made in recruiting key employees: (1) not properly defining job requirements or what it would take to be successful on the job; (2) unintentionally limiting sources for candidates; (3) failing to interview candidates thoroughly; (4) falling for the halo effect; (5) wishful thinking (especially when desperate to fill a position); (6) ignoring intuition; and (7) failing to check references.

RHR International. (1991). The psychological assessment of top executives:
An interview-based approach. In C. P. Hansen & K. A. Conrad (Eds.),
A handbook of psychological assessment in business (pp. 131-139).
New York: Quorum Books.

This handbook chapter focuses on assessments at the CEO and executive or senior vice-president levels. The authors argue that assessing candidates for jobs at this level is different in fundamental ways from assessing
candidates for jobs at lower levels in the organization for two reasons. First,
the fit between the incumbent and other senior executives, the company
culture, and the company's past and future is critical. Second, skill and
experience at this level are assumed; how an executive goes about employing
this skill and experience is the important factor.

The authors recommend a three-stage process in assessment:
preassessment, assessment, and feedback. During preassessment, an organizational analysis is done (including information about the company, its leadership, its industry, and its marketplace). This is condensed into a summary of
key performance demands similar to a job description. Next, the selection
committee is prepared for their interviews with the individuals to be assessed
(including judgments they might want to make, information they need to
make those judgments, and questions to ask to solicit that information).
During the assessment phase, a measure of the person is taken relative to the
dimensions identified in the preassessment phase through interviews. In the
postassessment phase, the first step is to enhance the ownership of the
decision-making process by the selection committee and clarify with them
what must be done to ensure the success of the selected individual. Finally,
the individual is prepared for success in the new position by stimulating
interest in and motivation toward self-development in critical areas.

Ross, M. B. (1989, November). CEO selection: Getting it right. *Trustee, 13,*
p. 24.

The author lists the steps necessary for the board to select a CEO. These
are: (1) organizational assessment and development of a strategic plan;
(2) development of a CEO job specification; (3) development of a CEO
evaluation system; (4) use of an employee contract spelling out the compensation package, management goals, the frequency and method of performance

evaluation, and a severance agreement; and (5) development of a fair and competitive compensation plan.

Sorcher, M. (1985). *Predicting executive success: What it takes to make it into senior management*. New York: John Wiley & Sons, 280 pages.

Using his own experiences as well as those of hundreds of very senior managers (CEOs, presidents, senior vice presidents, and executive vice presidents) in a variety of businesses, Sorcher describes a process for identifying and evaluating candidates for top-level positions. To begin, Sorcher estimates that one-third of selections at the top are unsuccessful, another third are not doing all that well, and one-third are extremely effective. Then he outlines four principles that underlie his assumptions regarding increasing the accuracy of prediction in selection: (1) Prediction is a continuous process from early identification to imminent appointment. (2) Selection should use a multidimensional process with tangible criteria for evaluating abilities and accomplishments. (3) Situational predictions (for example, questions aimed at anticipated situations and circumstances) are required to improve the odds of future success. (4) The process for the selection at the top should be led by an individual who has no vested interest in the outcome.

Sorcher, with a clear preference for internal selections, outlines his process in eight chapters. First, he describes the responsibilities for selection, including who the selectors are and what their roles are. He outlines when the selection process should begin and explains the need for quality control and assuring a continuous supply of candidates. In the next two chapters, he addresses early identification (including early identification using college recruiting, assessment centers, sponsors and supervisors, and performance appraisals) and career-planning issues.

The heart of the book is in the next few chapters: selecting potential candidates through testing the candidates, narrowing the pool, and then finally making the best fit to the position. These chapters discuss the need for measurable criteria and behavioral observations, the importance of and how to do group evaluations, differentiating between candidates and identifying flaws, and making the big decision.

Valentine, J. A. (1991, November). A strategy for executive staffing. *The Journal of Business Strategy*, pp. 56-58.

The author suggests that the failure of a newly hired executive to perform on the job may not be due to his or her shortcomings, but to management's; the weakness may lie in the strategy that affected the personnel change. To shape the process, Valentine recommends a four-step process: (1) Start with an evaluation of the position (and not of the people). (2) Create the ideal candidate required to fill such a position. (3) Spread the recruiting "net" for locating the needed talent. (4) Finally, contact the candidates and assess their potential contributions.

Van Clieaf, M. S. (1992). Strategy and structure follow people: Improving organizational performance through effective executive search. *Human Resource Planning, 15*(1), 33-46.

The author questions the assumption that the generalist general manager can effectively run any business. Additionally, he suggests that personality and temperament are not important (unless executive behavior is really destructive). Instead, during selection, selectors should determine the intended business strategy of the organization, the stage or complexity of the organization, and critical success factors needed. Executive search should be aligned with these drivers.

Specific Methods

Baehr, M. E. (1992). *Predicting success in higher-level positions: A guide to the system for testing and evaluation of potential.* New York: Quorum Books, 271 pages.

This book outlines a procedure for selecting managers from first-level line managers through executives using a procedure called the System for Testing and Evaluation of Potential (STEP). STEP is based on the two interlocking procedures of measuring the demands of the job and the qualifications of applicants. Potential is defined as the empirically derived estimate of "fit" between the requirements of the functions to be performed in the position and the abilities, skills, and attributes that the individual has. The book outlines the development of the procedures and tests used in STEP, reliability and validity tests, and how to apply STEP.

Howard, A. (1992, November). *Selecting executives for the 21st century: Can assessment centers meet the challenge?* Paper presented at Executive Selection Conference, Center for Creative Leadership, Greensboro, NC, 32 pages.

Howard debunks seven assumptions regarding why assessment centers are not useful at the top of the organization. First, she contends that assessment-center dimensions are, in fact, not dated. The dimensions contain core constructs such as decision making, as well as ones that are more necessary in today's environment, including tolerance of uncertainty, social objectivity (a diversity dimension), and behavior flexibility. New dimensions have been and can be added, such as motivation to empower others and team development. Second, Howard argues that assessment centers have been validated against criteria beyond merely career progress, such as performance ratings, potential, wages, and training performance. Third, Howard points out that assessment centers have been used and been found to be valid for executive-level positions. However, the dimensions needed may be slightly different. For example, middle managers are expected to use sound judgment (make timely and sound decisions and make decisions under conditions of uncertainty) while executives are expected to use seasoned judgment (apply broad knowledge and seasoned experience); both are parts of the decision-making dimension.

Fourth, she argues that assessment centers can be used to predict performance in "idiosyncratic" jobs (for example, stable, start-up, turn-around). For example, start-ups require entrepreneurial orientation, visionary thinking, and so forth—all measurable in an assessment center. Further, she argues that perhaps constructs such as business-situation versatility or adaptability can be used to measure whether executives can meet the challenges of different situations. Fifth, she agrees that construct validity may be a problem but that it is fixable in a variety of ways, including using more than one assessor per exercise and better defining the different constructs. Sixth, Howard believes that assessment centers can be made to be user-friendly in a variety of ways using statistics, technology, and specialized (as opposed to generalized) training for the assessors. And finally, she contends that assessment centers already have an indirect impact at the top, through use in the lower levels. And despite excuses such as high cost and the capability of top executives to make good decisions on the behavior that they see every day, Howard believes that top executives, shaken by recent failures in organizational performance, will encourage new selection methods.

Howard, A., & Bray, D. W. (1988). *Managerial lives in transition: Advancing age and changing times*. New York: The Guilford Press, 462 pages.

This book outlines two longitudinal studies on movement into managerial ranks undertaken by AT&T. The first study, the Management Progress Study (MPS) began in 1955 and data collection continued for twenty years on the career paths of 422 white males (274 college recruits and 148 non-college recruits—with a total of 266 participants remaining throughout the duration of the study). The second study, the Management Continuity Study (MCS), began in 1977 and data collection continued for five years on the career paths of 391 college recruits with a more heterogeneous background including women, blacks, and Hispanics.

The book includes a substantial amount of statistical data, comparing and contrasting college to non-college recruits, men to women, whites to non-whites, managers who came of age in the 1950s to managers who came of age in the 1970s, and the well-adjusted with the less well-adjusted.

Using biographical data, interviews, paper-and-pencil inventories, and assessment centers, the authors explore what it takes to make it into management and how background, personality, skill, ability, adjustment, and social/cultural dimensions influence making it. In both samples a few of the predictors of later managerial success (as defined by movement upward into the managerial ranks) included the following: an intellectually stimulating family background, academic success and major, the desire to develop and improve oneself, job orientation and expectations, ambition, leadership motivation, cognitive ability, administrative ability, and interpersonal skills.

Judge, T. A., Cable, D. M., Boudreau, J. W., & Bretz, R. D., Jr. (1995). An empirical investigation of the predictors of executive career success. *Personnel Psychology, 48*, 485-519.

Using a random sample of 50% of the names on a large executive search firm's database, the authors asked 3,581 individuals about what variables predict executive career success in terms of both objective and subjective measures. The 1,388 responses revealed several variables, predicting two objective and two subjective measures of success. The objective measures are: (1) *Cash compensation.* The predicting variables included human capital (degree in business or law, performance ratings, Ivy League graduate, graduate degree, and educational quality); demographics (older, male, married, and spouse unemployed); motivation (hours worked, evenings worked, hours of work desired, ambition, and work centrality); as well as various organizational and industry/regional variables. (2) *Number of promotions.* This was predicted by similar variables, although the magnitude was weaker.

The two subjective measures of success are: (1) *Job satisfaction.* Predicting variables included human capital (educational quality); demographics (whites were less satisfied); motivation (evenings worked per month, hours of work desired, and lower ambition); and organizational success. (2) *Career satisfaction.* This was predicted by pay and promotions; demographics (younger, nonwhite, and those who devoted less time to dependent care); human capital (being an engineer, educational quality, performance ratings, and less tenure); motivation (lower ambition); organizational success; and industry variables.

Lindsey, E. H., Homes, V., & McCall, M. W., Jr. (1987). *Key events in executives' lives* (Rep. No. 32). Greensboro, NC: Center for Creative Leadership, 383 pages.

This technical report addresses the development of executives rather than specific issues around selection. The primary research question was "How do we develop adequate depth in executive talent to run the business in years to come?" Data were collected from 191 high-potential and successful executives from six corporations (86 interviews and 112 open-ended surveys). Successful was defined here in terms of career advancement. Selection for inclusion was non-random. Using retrospective self-report interviews and surveys, these executives gave 616 descriptions of key events that led to lasting changes in them as managers and 1,547 descriptions of lessons learned from those events.

The 616 key events were clustered into 16 events categories, and the 1,547 lessons were clustered into 31 lesson categories using inductive analysis from the interview data. These were expanded to 17 events categories and 34 lesson categories from the open-ended surveys.

The basic finding of the research is: It is not the specific job or the career tools (for example, job rotation, mentoring programs, career pathing) that matter; what matters is the important developmental events on the job and what is learned from these events.

McCall, M. W., Jr., Lombardo, M. M., & Morrison, A. M. (1988). *The lessons of experience: How successful executives develop on the job.* New York: Lexington Books, 210 pages.

The authors estimate that the cost of a failed executive is half-a-million dollars including the costs of selection, relocation, outplacement, and replacement (and not including the business costs of poor performance or poor morale). This classic book—which accompanies the above technical report by Lindsey, Homes, and McCall—emphasizes how to make the lessons of experience work.

Important job experiences and the lessons learned from them are described. Suggestions are given for ways managers can make more of these experiences and for ways that organizations can make use of them as development tools. In this way, organizations can produce a cadre of executives with the skills necessary to run the organization effectively.

Russell, C. J. (1990). Selecting top corporate leaders: An example of biographical information. *Journal of Management, 16*(1), 73-86.

The objective of this article was to describe and present preliminary data on the use of biographical information in the selection of top executives. Sixty-six male candidates were evaluated for positions as division general managers in a Fortune 50 firm. A job analysis by top-performing general managers revealed nine components critical to the GM job. Biographical information relating to these components was collected through interviews with candidates and their immediate superiors regarding accomplishments, disappointments, learnings, obstacles, assistance, conflicts, and so forth.

Additionally candidates spoke about career aspirations, formal development activities, self-perceptions, and other perceptions. These were used to rate candidates on each dimension and one overall dimension. Questionnaires on the nine dimensions were sent to subordinates, peers, and prior superiors. Criteria included two global performance ratings (fiscal and nonfiscal [these were not further defined]), as given annually by superiors, and amount of recent bonus received. Correlations demonstrated that two of the independent variables were related to bonus, and one was related to nonfiscal performance.

Ryan, A. M., & Sackett, P. R. (1987). A survey of individual assessment practices by I/O psychologists. *Personnel Psychology, 40,* 455-488.

This is a report of a survey sent to 1,001 members of the Society for Industrial and Organizational Psychology who indicated that they were interested in personnel selection, personnel evaluation, assessment, or personality assessment. The survey consisted of 103 questions (both multiple choice and open-ended) regarding background and general practice information, assessment methods, assessment content, assessment process and techniques, training requirements, and attitudes. The response rate was 31.6%, with 316 usable questionnaires returned.

Findings were that 163 practiced individual assessment; 153 did not (and only filled out part of the survey); and 25% did assessment for upper management. For organization and job assessment, assessors gather information on the job description, climate/culture, performance expectations, management style, why the organization wants the assessment, style and personality of the immediate supervisor, why/how past incumbents have succeeded or failed, and so forth.

Tools used for selection include personal history form (81%), ability tests (85%), personality inventories (85%), projective tests (50%), simulation exercises (32%), and interviews (94%). Other methods include reference checks, interviews with superiors and co-workers, contact at meals, surveys of management practices, and past performance information.

Raters assessed numerous dimensions. The top eight were interpersonal skills, judgment/analytical skill, organization and planning, intelligence, supervisory skills, emotional maturity, leadership, and energy/drive. To make their decisions, 56% relied purely on judgment, and 42% used both judgment and statistical procedures. Finally, most did not regularly empirically validate the process they used, and only 27% did follow-up on the individuals they assessed.

Sackett, P. R. (1992, November). *Personnel research and executive selection: Some contrasts between research and practice.* Paper presented at Executive Selection Conference, Center for Creative Leadership, Greensboro, NC, 15 pages.

Sackett outlines six issues on how researchers and practitioners differently approach selection. The difference in perspectives has caused practitioners to be increasingly skeptical about the use of psychologically based personnel-selection tools, especially in top management.

First, practitioners are interested in individual prediction or knowing whether a particular individual will perform on the job in question. Researchers typically interested in institutional prediction ask a very different question: "Will a group of individuals with higher levels of a characteristic outperform a group of individuals with lower levels?"

Second, researchers often study selection procedures in isolation. They don't look at the incremental value of various predictors. Thus little is known regarding who to select when each of three candidates score high on one of three predictors.

Third, research is often predictor-focused rather than performance-focused. Research concentrates on documenting the effectiveness of a particular selection device or construct, while criterion measures are chosen for reasons of convenience. This may result in only one aspect of job performance or in taking a global, rather than multidimensional, approach to performance measurement. However, different facets of performance may be related to different predictors.

Fourth, researchers often fail to distinguish between the constructs being measured and the methods by which they are measured. Instead of framing the question "Are these particular work experiences valid?", the question asked is "Is the interview a valid selection device?" The interview is an information-gathering method that can be used to collect a whole variety of information, some of which may be valid and others not.

Fifth, little research has been directed toward understanding the interaction between organizational characteristics and individual-difference methods under consideration. And finally, work experience is often not used in a sophisticated manner in research. Rather, it is often used as a moderator or in terms of seniority. However, quality and quantity of experience may be the most highly predictive measure, especially in top executives where such constructs as cognitive ability may have low variability. Sackett recommends exploring and improving upon individual assessment approaches to help rectify these differences.

Shackleton, V., & Newell, S. (1991). Management selection: A comparative survey of methods used in top British and French companies. *Journal of Occupational Psychology, 64,* 23-36.

The object of this paper is twofold. First, the authors explored how British selection practices have changed in a five-year timeframe. They replicated, in 1989, a 1984 survey (completed by a different set of authors) with a survey on 73 (out of 120) organizations. Second, they did a cross-national comparison between British (n=73) and French companies (n=52 out of 120).

Organizations were randomly drawn from The Times 1000 and Les 200 Premieres Groupes des Echos (both indices are similar to the Fortune 500). Companies used application forms, references, personality tests, cognitive tests, and, to a lesser extent, assessment centers, biodata, handwriting analysis, and astrology.

Results suggest that British companies are starting to use "valid and reliable" selection techniques—such as psychological tests, biodata, and assessment centers—to a greater extent. In terms of the cross-national comparison, large companies in both countries are more likely to use the more "respectable" methods (for example, less reliance on such methods as astrology, though graphology is still used to some extent in France) for selection; Britain, however, seems to be ahead of France. The authors suggest that there is room for improvement in both countries.

White, R. P., & DeVries, D. L. (1990, Winter). Making the wrong choice: Failure in the selection of senior-level managers. *Issues & Observations, 10*(1), 1-6.

This article asserts that one-third to one-half of those chosen for senior executive positions are subsequently seen as disappointments. Why are selections so often unsuccessful? White and DeVries point to three factors: Jobs at senior levels are very difficult, selection is made on narrow grounds, and assessment tools are weak. The authors contend that selection is often narrow, focusing on technical competence and track record. Less emphasis is placed on other qualities (such as the capacity to learn and personal values) or on understanding the job itself. In terms of assessment, the authors recommend continuous, systematic, and multidimensional assessment throughout the careers of executives.

Other Issues

Gioia, D. A., & Longnecker, C. O. (1994). Delving into the dark side: The politics of executive appraisal. *Organizational Dynamics, 22,* 47-58.

The authors assert that politics plays a sinister role in executive performance appraisals. Politics in executive appraisal refers to any deliberate attempt on the part of a higher-ranking executive to enhance, control, or protect self or organizational interests through the appraisal of subordinate executives.

The authors conducted interviews of eighty-two executives from eight large manufacturing and service firms. All were managers of managers and reported to at least one higher-level manager. Interviews were concerned with the nature of politics in executive appraisal and the consequences of politics.

The nature of politics centered on five areas: (1) Politics is prevalent in appraisal, and the higher one rises in the organization, the more political the appraisal process becomes. (2) Because of the dynamic ambiguous nature of managerial work, appraisals are susceptible to political manipulation. (3) Performance is not necessarily the bottom line in the appraisal process; instead the boss's agenda, the executive's reputation, and the company's political climate play a role. (4) Senior executives have extraordinary latitude in evaluating subordinates' performance. (5) Executive appraisal is a "political" tool used to control people and resources—interviewees feel they are being manipulated for someone else's benefit.

The consequences of political executive appraisal include: (1) undermining organizational goals and performance; (2) compromising the link between executive performance and outcomes; (3) inhibiting executive development; (4) begetting politics in the rest of the organization; and (5) exposing an organization to litigation when executives are terminated.

Hitt, M. A., & Barr, S. H. (1989). Managerial selection decision models: Examination of configural cue processing. *Journal of Applied Psychology, 74*(1), 53-61.

The purpose of this research was to examine what determines job-applicant favorability and recommended starting salary in a controlled experiment designed to represent a realistic and complex working environment. The researchers hypothesized that managers would use job-relevant (education and years of experience) and job-irrelevant (sex, race, age) factors in evaluating candidates; that participants' demographic characteristics would affect their evaluations; that there would be a great many interactions; and that race, sex, and age would affect starting salaries, even after taking into account human-capital variables (years experience, education, level of position).

Sixty-eight managers (44 male, 24 female) viewed one set (out of four) of information (videotapes and applications) on sixteen job candidates and evaluated them on favorability and estimated starting salary. Age, sex, race, experience, education, and level of job were manipulated. Results demonstrated that both job-relevant and job-irrelevant cues were used, that rater demographics were important, and that decision models were complex (as seen by the number of interactions). Only candidate sex had an impact on starting salary recommendations.

Kets de Vries, M. (1988, January). The dark side of CEO succession. *Harvard Business Review, 88*(1), 56-60.

Kets de Vries suggests that some CEOs and other key players (board members, top-management team members) have a hard time dealing with CEO succession and retirement. Thus, they may avoid taking real action, thereby sabotaging a succession. He analyzes several hidden forces that may disrupt the succession.

In stepping down, the CEO contends with two problems: the realization of one's mortality and the fear of losing power. In selecting a successor, the CEO looks for a perfect solution, and must contend with "playing favorites" when singling out someone from the group as a successor. Both of these forces often lead the CEO to look outside the organization. Finally, when the succession takes place, the status quo is disrupted. The new CEO must deal with the tendency of people to idealize the past. At the same time, during succession (or any "crisis" atmosphere), people have a tendency to need strong leaders. This allows for a honeymoon period for the new CEO, which may eventually turn into disillusionment as the new CEO is unable to meet exaggerated expectations.

Ruderman, M. N., & Ohlott, P. J. (1990). *Traps and pitfalls in the judgment of executive potential* (Rep. No. 141). Greensboro, NC: Center for Creative Leadership, 47 pages.

The purpose of this report is to outline the filters, screens, and shortcuts people use to cope with the normal flood of daily stimuli, and demonstrate how such processes as human resources decisions and the identification of talent can be biased by these information-processing strategies. These include framing, which influences the number and type of people screened; stereotyping, which influences how individuals store and recall information; confusing evaluation and prediction, which influences how individuals view tests of performance; and people tending to rely on their own personal experience or verbal recommendations of others, rather than written summaries. Ruderman and Ohlott also outline why these biases continue and how to work within the biases to create better review systems.

Ruderman, M. N., & Ohlott, P. J. (1994). *The realities of management promotion: An investigation of factors influencing the promotion of managers in three major companies* (Rep. No. 157). Greensboro, NC: Center for Creative Leadership, 57 pages.

The objective of this study was to understand how actual promotions are made. The authors conducted an exploratory study of how sixty-four promotions actually occurred in three companies. Although they found that promotions are based on individual efforts and abilities, they found that context—such as being in the right place for the right opportunity, using promotions as signals, and using them for developmental purposes—also played a part in promotions in 81% of the cases.

Additionally, they found that the nature of the job influenced, but did not determine, the selection criteria for the positions; that there was often only one person considered for the job; and that hiring managers relied on intuition instead of formally collected data. They also found that type of promotion and the reason for the promotion varied both within the company (possible promotions include: developmental, promotion in place, promotions with no obvious optimal candidate, long-term staffing goals, and reorganizations) and between companies.

Zald, M. N. (1965). Who shall rule? A political analysis of succession in a
    large welfare organization. *Pacific Sociological Review, 8,* 52-60.

This classic article suggests that succession should be studied more broadly than just using a "career" or "effectiveness" approach. Succession also must be seen as a basic political process involving components of power, mechanisms of election which may favor one kind of successor over another, and basic choices of organizational goals.

Executive Performance After Selection

This chapter is divided into three sections: (1) transitions into the position; (2) success and failure on the job; and (3) transitions out of the position.

The annotations here are useful for those who have to live with the selection once it has taken place. The books and articles in each of the three sections represent programs of research, which allow the reader to more easily draw conclusions about transitioning into the job, success and failure, and transitioning out of the job.

The first section addresses executives' movement into the job in terms of the executive taking charge (Gabarro, 1988; Nicholson & West, 1989), changes the executive makes (Bhambri & Greiner, 1989; Gabarro, 1987; Greiner & Bhambri, 1989), and organizational components (Nicholson & West, 1989; Raben & Heilpern, 1994). The section on success and failure on the job addresses differences between successful managers, effective managers (Luthans, Hodgetts, & Rosenkrantz, 1988), and those who derail (Kaplan, Drath, & Kofodimos, 1991; Leslie & Van Velsor, 1996; Lombardo & McCauley, 1988; Lombardo, Ruderman, & McCauley, 1988; Morrison, White, & Van Velsor, 1992). The section on transitions out of the position addresses the conditions under which top executives are asked to leave (Boeker, 1992; Fredrickson, Hambrick, & Baumrin, 1988), the reactions of the executive (Sonnenfeld, 1988), and reactions of others in the organization (Friedman & Saul, 1991).

What do these readings have to say about a successful executive-selection process? They demonstrate that the selection process does not end once the job offer is accepted. It can take an executive up to two-and-one-half years to master the job. How he or she attempts to master it can be predicted from personality, style, and prior experiences. Once on the job at these levels, what it takes to be successful changes and what once worked for the executive in previous lower-level jobs no longer works. The executive must change to remain successful or derail.

For those executives who fail, the process is complex for the organization and for the individual. For these reasons, it is in the best interest of the organizational members to provide socialization experiences to the new executive (especially outsiders) that introduce him or her to the top-management team. It is also helpful to provide the new executive early on with information about the strategic direction, performance, and culture of the organization.

What further information is needed to help with successful selection? The programs of research presented here are some of the most coherent found in executive selection. However, they remain at the conceptual, theoretical level. There is little information on how to ensure a smooth transition on the job at high levels, either for the individual executive or for the organization.

Helpful information for the executive might include how to prepare for the job, what issues will have to be dealt with the first few years (for example, what kinds of activities will take their time and energy, what are their primary functions), how to make an impact, and how to gain acceptance and support. For the organization, helpful information might include how to socialize the executive into his or her position, how to clearly define expectations, what situations are most developmental for the executive, and how to give feedback early in the executive's tenure.

Transitions into the Position

Bhambri, A., & Greiner, L. E. (1989). *A conditional theory of CEO intervention and strategic change* (Tech. Rep.). Los Angeles: University of
Southern California, 48 pages.

The underlying premise of this report is that the new CEO's personality,
style, and prior company performance determine his or her propensity to
change and the type of intervention necessary; also, that the match between
the CEO's type of intervention and the surrounding organization determines
success or failure in implementation and performance. Intervention success is
defined as both the attainment of change and improved financial performance.
The authors outline the following: what characteristics lead to which change
interventions; the scope and style of the change intervention; organization
receptivity to the change; and environmental contingencies. Propositions are
developed regarding these issues.

Gabarro, J. J. (1987). *The dynamics of taking charge.* Boston: Harvard
Business School Press, 204 pages.

Using seventeen in-depth interviews with general managers through
chief executives, Gabarro outlines the process by which a manager establishes
mastery and influence in a new assignment. Mastery is acquiring a grounded
understanding of the organization, tasks, people, environment, and problems.
Influence means having an impact on the organization and its structure,
practices, and performance. The process takes two to two-and-one-half years
for U.S. senior-level managers and includes taking hold (3-6 months, characterized by the first change effort), immersion (4-11 months, little change
activity), reshaping (3-6 months, characterized by another major change
effort), consolidation (3-9 months, small changes), and refinement stage
(manager is no longer "taking charge," relatively minor organizational
change).

Additionally, Gabarro analyzed the data by comparing successful
versus unsuccessful managers. Unsuccessful managers were those terminated
within three years of succession for failure to meet top management's performance expectations. Patterns associated with failure include both being
industry outsiders and having poor working relations with superiors, peers,
and subordinates. Managers who failed approached tasks in a solitary fashion,

used teams less, and made changes perceived as inappropriate or ineffective (due to partial or incorrect diagnoses of the problems or because the changes were badly implemented by people who did not support them).

Gabarro, J. J. (1988). Executive leadership and succession: The process of taking charge. In D. C. Hambrick (Ed.), *The executive effect: Concepts and methods for studying top managers* (pp. 237-268). Greenwich, CT: JAI Press, Inc.

Gabarro proposes a "taking charge" process in executive succession that takes over eighteen months. The taking-charge process includes the following: (1) succession variables such as successor characteristics (insider-outsider, industry-relevant experience, style and predispositions, and so forth); (2) situational factors (for example, turnaround or normal succession) and prearrival activities (for example, negotiating expectations); (3) the actual taking-charge process, which has several stages as well as several work factors, including cognitive work (learning and developing), organizational work (for example, building a cohesive team), and interpersonal work (developing effective working relationships); and (4) outcomes, including gaining understanding and mastery, developing a power base and acceptance as a leader, and impact on organizational performance (positive or negative).

Greiner, L. E., & Bhambri, A. (1989). New CEO intervention and dynamics of deliberate strategic change. *Strategic Management Journal, 10,* 67-86.

Although growing evidence in the executive-succession literature suggests that new CEOs often attempt to introduce strategic change when starting their jobs, little documentation is available on the internal dynamics of these interventions or their success. This article presents a case study where a new CEO succeeds at strategic change using a "comprehensive/ collaborative" intervention approach (big change, using the entire top-management team). The authors develop a set of propositions and a theoretical framework.

Nicholson, N., & West, M. (1989). Transitions, work, histories, and careers. In M. B. Arthur, D. T. Hall, & B. S. Lawrence (Eds.), *Handbook of career theory* (pp. 181-201). New York: Cambridge University Press.

Nicholson and West propose a theory of work-role transitions at two levels of analysis: individual and organizational. The theory is based on their belief that the integrity and meaning of careers (or *work histories* in their terminology) should be studied empirically through a fine-graded analysis of transitions and the periods between them. It is based on four assumptions: Change is the norm; the last stage of one cycle is the first of the next one; the content of the experience at one stage will strongly influence the content of experience at subsequent stages; and experiences have distinctive qualities at each stage. For each level of analysis, the theory includes: preparation, encounter, adjustment, and stabilization.

Preparation includes the processes of expectation and anticipation before the change. At the individual level, this is difficult to study as the onset of many transitions is unpredictable. However, the authors' research does suggest that individuals have a positive anticipation of future challenges and new experience. At the organizational level, preparation includes recruitment and transfer processes.

Encounter is the affect and sense-making during the first days or weeks of job tenure. At the individual level this is ranked as stressful, though it is positive stress associated with challenge, freedom, and so on, except in the case of downward status and job loss. At the organizational level, encounter includes socialization and induction practices along with the demographic make-up of the organization.

Adjustment is personal and role development to reduce person-job misfit. At the individual level, employees change both themselves and their jobs. At the organizational level, adjustment includes job design, training, and supervision.

Stabilization (which leads to preparation) is the settled connection between person and role. At the individual level, stability and change can take place in a variety of forms. In Nicholson and West's research, opportunities for radical moves were more common than incremental moves. At the organizational level, stabilization includes information and management systems that regulate and control performance.

Raben, C. S., & Heilpern, J. D. (1994, March). Breaking in the new CEO. *The Corporate Board*, pp. 4-6.

The authors suggest that the board of directors should take responsibility for introducing the new CEO (especially one selected from outside the company) into the organization, by providing him or her with information about strategic direction, performance, culture, and the senior-management team. This introduction should occur early and should take place at board meetings as well as at one-on-one discussions.

Success and Failure on the Job

Kaplan, R. E., Drath, W. H., & Kofodimos, J. R. (1991). *Beyond ambition: How driven managers can lead better and live better.* San Francisco: Jossey-Bass, 269 pages.

This book presents a theory on executive character and development. It is based on the premise that the way executives are as people matters greatly to the leadership they offer; and therefore, executives improve as leaders by growing as human beings. The theory focuses on a particular characteristic, *expansiveness*, which can be a strength or (when carried to extremes) a derailment factor in executives.

Expansiveness is the drive to personal mastery and achievement, the ambition for it, the willingness to expend great energy in its pursuit, the willingness to push other people hard to attain it, and the hunger for the rewards that come with it. Those with an expansive personality may strive to attain a position in the executive suite as a fulfillment of their needs for high position, socioeconomic status, power and prestige, and prerogatives and special treatment.

The executive job and career track carry with them expectations for the very sort of expansiveness that leads these individuals to seek high positions in the first place. However, once in the executive suite, expansive individuals need to become less single-minded in order to be successful at marshaling support, creativity, and team effort.

To develop this theory, researchers collected intensive data on forty-two predominantly white American male top-level executives (CEO to one level below general manager), using multiple perspectives and multiple settings, done over multiple time periods. Using case studies, they describe the expansive executive and show how organizations can help executives develop and balance their character on the road to managerial excellence.

Leslie, J. B., & Van Velsor, E. (1996). *A look at derailment today: North America and Europe* (Rep. No. 169). Greensboro, NC: Center for Creative Leadership, 76 pages.

This report is a replication and extension of the Center for Creative Leadership's original derailment research (see this section, Lombardo & McCauley, 1988; Lombardo, Ruderman, & McCauley, 1988) applied to contemporary derailed and successful executives in the U.S. and Europe. The new study was conducted in order to discover if the same factors were causing derailment five years later in today's U.S. organizations and whether the derailment literature extended to senior executives in Europe.

Twenty primarily white middle-aged senior executives in the U.S. and forty-two English-speaking middle-aged senior executives from Europe (Belgium, France, Germany, Italy, Spain, and the United Kingdom) were interviewed. Participants were asked to describe two managers that they knew well, one of whom made it to the top and one who had derailed.

Analyses indicate that the same derailment themes and success themes that arose in the original studies are still present today in both samples, although the importance of those themes is shifting. The derailment themes were: problems with interpersonal relationships, failure to meet business objectives, inability to build and lead a team, and inability to change or adapt during a transition. The success themes were: being ambitious, establishing strong relationships, showing consistently high performance, exhibiting team-building and leadership skills, being intelligent, willing to take risks, able to adapt, and being a problem-solver.

Lombardo, M. M., & McCauley, C. D. (1988). *The dynamics of management derailment* (Rep. No. 34). Greensboro, NC: Center for Creative Leadership, 34 pages.

Derailment occurs when a manager who was expected to go higher in the organization and who was judged to have the ability to do so is fired, demoted, or plateaued below the expected levels of achievement. In this study the primary research questions were: (1) Can the reasons for derailment be reduced to some basic clusters of flaws? (2) Are some flaws seen as more harmful to a manager's career than others? (3) Would the same flaws threaten careers in any company? (4) What is the relationship between flaws and managerial skills? (5) Are certain flaws more likely to affect a manager's ability to handle particular jobs? (6) Are derailed and successful managers viewed differently before the fact?

To answer these questions, 335 managers from eight large corporations completed a 360-degree-feedback instrument in development at the Center for Creative Leadership, later to be called Benchmarks®. The subordinate managers were at the executive level, middle managers, and first-line supervisors. Six basic flaws arose using factor analysis: (1) problems with interpersonal relationships; (2) difficulty in molding a staff; (3) difficulty in making strategic transitions; (4) lack of follow-through; (5) overdependence on a boss or mentor; and (6) strategic disagreements with higher management.

Using regression analysis, the three most "fatal" flaws (all six flaws were significantly related to derailment) were: (1) difficulty in molding a staff; (2) difficulty in making strategic transitions; and (3) lack of follow-through. Although the flaws existed in all eight organizations in the sample, no two organizations had the same pattern of relationships between flaws and derailment, suggesting that different flaws are viewed differently in different settings.

Particular flaws were related to particular skills. For example, difficulty in molding a staff was associated with poor hiring decisions, poor climate, and poor leadership of subordinates. The managerial-skill-oriented flaws were detrimental to handling most jobs, but mattered the most in the more challenging jobs (and thus may not emerge until the executive reaches the higher levels of the organization). Overdependence was most associated with the inability to handle large-scope changes; and problems with interpersonal relationships were linked with the inability to handle jobs requiring persuasion and the development of working relationships.

Finally, were the derailed and promoted managers viewed differently before the fact? Although the sample size assessed here was small, preliminary data suggest that a lack of management skills (such as strategic thinking and follow-through), combined with a lack of personal qualities (such as flexibility), and moving into a challenging job situation may cause the derailment to occur.

Lombardo, M. M., Ruderman, M. N., & McCauley, C. D. (1988). Explanations of success and derailment in upper-level management positions. *Journal of Business and Psychology, 2,* 199-216.

The primary research question in this study was: In what ways do decision-makers perceive derailed executives differently from successful executives? Derailed managers were defined as those who had been terminated. Successful managers were those who were seen as promotable or who had superior performance in their present position. This study used bosses' or peer ratings on the *Executive Inventory* (Lombardo, 1985) for 169 mid- to upper-level male managers in a multinational company (90% response rate).

The inventory was factor-analyzed into eight scales: handling business complexity; directing, motivating, and developing subordinates; honor; drive for excellence; organizational savvy; composure; sensitivity; and staffing. The successful group scored significantly lower (showing higher competence) on each scale.

Luthans, F., Hodgetts, R. M., & Rosenkrantz, S. A. (1988). *Real managers.* Cambridge, MA: Ballinger, 192 pages.

This book presents an empirical study designed to answer three questions: (1) What do real managers do in real organizations? (2) What do successful managers do? (3) What do effective managers do?

Successful managers were defined according to their tenure in their organizations. CEOs were also defined as successful. Effective managers were defined by creating an index of the following measures: (1) organizational unit effectiveness in terms of quantity and quality of performance (Mott Organizational Effectiveness Questionnaire); (2) subordinate satisfaction (Job Diagnostic Index); and (3) subordinate organizational commitment (Organizational Commitment Questionnaire).

The authors defined what managers do, using observational methods. On average, managers spend 29% of their time in routine communications (exchanging information and handling paperwork); 32% of their time doing traditional management (planning, decision making, and controlling); 20% of their time doing human resources management (motivating/reinforcing, disciplining/punishing, managing conflict, staffing, training/developing); and 19% of their time networking (interacting with outsiders/politicking).

Successful managers spend 48% of their time networking; 28% of their time in routine communications; 13% of their time doing traditional management; and 11% of their time doing human resources management. Effective managers spend 45% of their time in routine communications; 27% of their time doing human resources management; 15% of their time doing traditional management functions; and 12% of their time networking.

The 15 out of 178 managers who were defined as both successful and effective spent their time in activities approximately equal to time spent by real managers.

Morrison, A. M., White, R. P., & Van Velsor, E. (1992). *Breaking the glass ceiling: Can women reach the top of America's largest corporations?* (Updated ed.). Reading, MA: Addison-Wesley, 231 pages.

The three-year study of female executives documented in this book replicates research from the Center for Creative Leadership's lessons-of-experience (see Lindsey, Homes, & McCall, 1987, in the chapter "Doing Selection and Prediction") and derailment work (see Lombardo and colleagues under this heading). Researchers interviewed seventy-six successful women at high levels on the factors that determine success or derailment in the corporate environment.

Researchers also interviewed another twenty-two higher-level executives, sixteen men and six women, and asked them to describe in detail two women executives, one who was successful and one who derailed.

In the derailment segment, six major factors were found to lead to success for women managers: help from above; a track record of achievement; desire to succeed; ability to manage subordinates; willingness to take career risks; and the ability to be tough, decisive, and demanding. Three major factors were found to lead to derailment for women managers: the inability to adapt, wanting too much, and performance problems. Women who succeed also have some "extras" including credibility and presence, strong advocacy, and outright luck.

In terms of lessons learned from key events in these women's careers that led to success or derailment, the authors suggested the following: learn the ropes, take control of one's own career, build confidence, rely on others, go for the bottom line, and integrate life and work.

Transitions out of the Position

Boeker, W. (1992). Power and managerial dismissal: Scapegoating at the top. *Administrative Science Quarterly, 37,* 400-421.

This study examines the influence that chief executive officers, owners, and boards of directors have over the dismissal process. Hypotheses are that dismissal of CEOs is more likely when organizational performance is poor and the power of the CEO is low. But when CEO power is high, members of the top-management team are more likely to be dismissed.

Power is defined in this study as residing with (1) the proportion of the board of directors who are insiders, (2) those appointed by the CEO, and (3) the CEO's proportion of firm membership (the rest of the firm membership being dispersed among others). Performance is defined by creating a proportion of two-year annual sales growth to average sales for the semiconductor industry. Dismissal is defined as an unexpected leaving (such as retirement, illness, or death) as indicated by marketing research firms.

The study used sixty-seven organizations over a twenty-two-year period to examine the likelihood of CEO and top-management dismissal as a result of organizational performance and the distribution of power in the organization. Powerful CEOs were found less likely than less-powerful chief executives to be dismissed during performance downturns. Instead, top managers were replaced.

Fredrickson, J. W., Hambrick, D. C., & Baumrin, S. (1988). A model of CEO dismissal. *Academy of Management Review, 13*(2), 255-270.

Although an organization's performance affects the dismissal of a CEO, past research suggests that the relationship is small. The authors propose a model that suggests social and political factors (such as the board of directors' expectations and attributions, the board's allegiances and values, the availability of alternative candidates, and the power of the CEO) mediate the relationship between performance and dismissal. Objective determinants of these constructs are identified including characteristics of the board, the organization, the industry, the CEO, and the CEO's predecessor.

Friedman, S. D., & Saul, K. (1991). A leader's wake: Organization member
    reactions to CEO succession. *Journal of Management, 17*(3), 619-642.

The object of this article is to examine how the context and content of
CEO succession affects the reactions of organization members. Using a
questionnaire answered by human resources professionals in 222 Fortune 500
firms (response rate of 24%), the influence of presuccession financial performance, predecessor tenure, why the CEO left, and successor origin was
assessed on postsuccession disruption, management turnover, and company
morale.

Presuccession performance had no influence on the three dependent
variables. Length of predecessor tenure was negatively related to morale but
positively related to executive turnover (opposite of that predicted). CEO
successions due to board initiation or CEO disability led to greater disruption
while CEO-initiated successions (either expected or unexpected) did not.
Board removal of a predecessor raised morale. Finally, outside successions
resulted in greater disruption and turnover but did not have an impact on
company morale.

Sonnenfeld, J. (1988). *The hero's farewell: What happens when CEOs retire.*
    New York: Oxford University Press, 320 pages.

Sonnenfeld studies the half of the succession equation often neglected
by most literature: the leaving of the incumbent leader. He builds the case that
corporate leaders embody the American hero myth to themselves, the organizations they run, and society at large.

Business heroes often rise from humble origins, have triumphed over
major career setbacks, have made sweeping strategic visions in their own
firms that are copied by others, have a remarkable knack for self-promotion,
and have a sense of civic responsibility.

Heroes believe that they have earned their stature through their deeds
and sacrifice. They don't realize until their retirement that their position is, in
part, a social creation. Two factors are barriers to the heroes' exit: their heroic
stature and their fulfillment of their heroic mission.

Using twelve sources of data including interviews with fifty recently
retired CEOs and their family members and work associates, Sonnenfeld
divided departure styles into four types: the "monarch" who does not retire
but dies or is forcefully removed from office; the "general" who retires

reluctantly but comes back to save the firm; the "ambassador" who retires but retains a lesser role as mentor or consultant; and the "governor" who retires and leaves the firm completely to do other things.

Organizational Outcomes

This chapter is divided into two sections: (1) outcomes attributable to individual executives (most often the CEO); and (2) outcomes attributable to the top-executive team.

The reasons for successful selection processes are illustrated, information that can be useful to all who are interested in executive selection. Although early research suggests that the influence of top executives may be small (Lieberson & O'Connor, 1972; Salancik & Pfeffer, 1977), other subsequent theory and research demonstrates that CEOs and other high-performing executives (Barrick, Day, Lord, & Alexander, 1991; Day & Lord, 1988; Levinson, 1994; Thomas, 1988; Zajac, 1990) as well as top-management teams (Eisenhardt & Schoonhoven, 1990; Hambrick & Mason, 1984; Murray, 1989) can make an impact on the bottom line, although the relationship may be complex (Finkelstein & Hambrick, 1990; Haleblian & Finkelstein, 1993; Hambrick & D'Aveni, 1992; Jackson, 1992; Scully, Sims, Olian, Schnell, & Smith, 1990).

For CEOs, organizational performance is higher when CEO compensation is monitored to a moderate degree (Tosi & Gomez-Mejia, 1994). Additionally, successions have an impact on reputation of the firm (in terms of such things as stock price) (Beatty & Zajac, 1987) and mortality (Haveman, 1993).

In the case of top-management teams, composition of the team may affect the bottom line through such mechanisms as innovation (Bantel & Jackson, 1989) and strategic change (Wiersema & Bantel, 1992).

What do these readings have to say about a successful executive-selection process? They demonstrate that individual executives and top-management teams have an impact on the bottom line. One article estimates that a high-performing executive has a 15% higher (in terms of dollars) impact than the average executive (Barrick et al., 1991). The cost of a failed executive may be as much as one-half-million dollars including the costs of selection, relocation, outplacement, and replacement (not including the business costs of poor performance or poor morale). (See McCall, Lombardo, & Morrison, 1988, in the "Doing Selection and Prediction" chapter.)

One learning to take away from these readings is that selecting a successful executive—as opposed to one who will ultimately fail or one who can get the job done but does not excel—is important. Spending resources, such as time and effort, to do the selection well is worth the effort.

What further information is needed to help with successful selection? Although the research here demonstrates that executives and top-management teams matter, there is little research regarding what leaders and teams do that affects performance and the bottom line. Additionally, there is little agreement on how to measure organizational effectiveness. Research is needed to explore different indicators of organizational effectiveness and where and how we would expect the top person and the top team to have an impact.

Attributable to CEOs

Barrick, M. R., Day, D. V., Lord, R. G., & Alexander, R. A. (1991). Assessing the utility of executive leadership. *Leadership Quarterly, 2*(1), 9-22.

Using utility analysis, the authors demonstrate that a high-performing executive has a substantial impact (in terms of dollars) on the economic performance of Fortune 500 companies—15% higher than the average performing executive. The value of these performance differences is expected to exceed 25 million dollars (after taxes) for a Fortune 500 company. Additionally, the average effect sizes predicted by financial analysts are consistent with the effect sizes computed in other similar studies, suggesting consistency of impact.

Beatty, R. P., & Zajac, E. J. (1987). CEO change and firm performance in large corporations: Succession effects and manager effects. *Strategic Management Journal, 8*, 305-317.

This article hypothesizes that stock price and systematic risk of a firm is related to the announcement of a CEO change. Using a cross-sectional/ longitudinal research design with a sample of 209 firms (184 insider and 25 outsider; 34 anticipated, 40 unanticipated, and 110 "can't tell"), the authors found that the market in general reacts negatively to both insider and outsider succession events. However, unanticipated changes are related to a decrease in stock price, while anticipated changes are related to an increase in stock price (before and after the event announcement date). Evidence also suggests (although to a lesser degree) that succession has an impact on the systematic risk of a firm's stock.

In terms of the anticipated and unanticipated changes (as read from *The Wall Street Journal*), it is not the succession that is of primary importance but the investment community's perception of the succession.

Day, D. V., & Lord, R. G. (1988). Executive leadership and organizational
    performance: Suggestions for a new theory and methodology. *Journal
    of Management, 14*(3), 453-464.

    The authors argue that past research that assesses the amount of impact
executive succession has on organization performance underestimates the true
impact. When correcting for methodological problems such as size, lag-time,
year effects, leader ability, order of entry, level of analysis, and dependent
variables, executive succession explains up to 45% of the variance in organizational outcomes.
    Additionally, the authors call for a theory specifying what top-level
leaders do that affects performance. Although not offering such a theory, they
suggest that a theory must avoid confusing levels or units of analysis, must
broaden beyond style and incorporate substance in relation to leadership, and
should incorporate new methodologies. Finally, they suggest that leadership
and organizational theory need to be integrated.

Haveman, H. A. (1993). Ghosts of managers past: Managerial succession and
    organizational mortality. *Academy of Management Journal, 36*(4),
    864-881.

    This study, using small organizations, investigated the effects of mana-
gerial succession on organizational mortality over time. The author predicted
that the effect of managerial succession on an organization would both
diminish as time passes and vary with organizational age. She also predicted
that the succession of the president would have a stronger impact on organizational mortality than the succession of other managers.
    Secondary data from the early American telephone industry (1900-
1917) were used to test these hypotheses. Results suggest that succession
increased organizational mortality, that these effects diminished over time,
and the relationship was stronger in younger organizations. Presidential exit
had a greater impact than turnover of other managers.

Levinson, H. (1994). Why behemoths fell: The psychological roots of corporate failure. *American Psychologist, 49*(5), 428-436.

Levinson suggests that the failure of many American corporations to
adapt to changed economic circumstances is due to psychological problems
of top executives. These include narcissism, unconscious recapitulation of
family dynamics in the organization, exacerbating dependency, psychologically illogical organization structure and compensation schemes, inadequate
management of change, and inability to recognize and manage cognitive
complexity.

Lieberson, S., & O'Connor, J. F. (1972). Leadership and organizational
performance: A study of large organizations. *American Sociological
Review, 37*, 117-130.

This classic article studies the influence of leadership on organizational
performance compared to the influence of such other factors as state of the
economy, the company's prime industry, and the company's position within
that industry; and studies the factors associated with interorganizational
differences in leadership impact. Data were gathered on 167 companies
located in thirteen different industries between 1946 and 1965.
Three indices of performance were used: sales, net earnings, and profit
margins. Leadership impact was studied using leadership changes—the
selection of a new president or chairman of the board. Results suggest that
leadership, though significant, played a small part in performance, with
environment playing a much stronger role.

Salancik, G. R., & Pfeffer, J. (1977). Constraints on administrator discretion:
The limited influence of mayors on city budgets. *Urban Affairs Quarterly, 12*(4), 475-498.

This classic article measures the mayoral influence on city expenditures, after taking into account city and year factors in thirty U.S. cities during
the years 1951-1968. Results demonstrate that the impact of the mayors on
variations in the city budget (ten categories) is relatively small compared to
the effect of the city itself. Mayoral influence accounted for between 5% (fire
expenditures) and 15.1% (parks and recreation and library expenditures), and

city influence accounted for between 54.5% (library) and 90.8% (property tax revenue).

Lag time, however, was not taken into account. For example, a mayor could set a policy that didn't have a noticeable effect for several years. Also, the possibility of a statistical artifact, because of the huge amount of variance between cities, has to be kept in mind.

Scully, J. A., Sims, H. P., Jr., Olian, J. D., Schnell, E. R., & Smith, K. A. (1994). Tough times make tough bosses: A meso-analysis of CEO leader behavior. *Leadership Quarterly, 5*(1), 59-83.

The study reported here investigated the relationship between firm financial performance and the leader behavior of the CEO approximately two years later. Using the four leader archetypes model developed in previous research by the authors, hypotheses predicted that leaders of poorly performing teams would be more likely to display behaviors in the "strongman" archetype (based on the authoritarian leadership style) and less likely to be transactional, visionary (transformational), or facilitative and consultative (the "SuperLeader").

Using interviews with CEOs and top-management team members of fifty-six firms (49% response rate), results demonstrated that there was a negative relationship between firm performance and authoritarian behaviors. Few relationships were found between the other archetypes and firm performance.

Thomas, A. B. (1988). Does leadership make a difference to organizational performance? *Administrative Science Quarterly, 33,* 388-400.

This article questions previous beliefs regarding the minor relationship between leadership and performance and suggests findings may be due to methodological weaknesses and incorrect analyses. The authors test these assumptions by studying the impact of CEOs on corporate performance using twelve large retail firms in the United Kingdom.

Corporate performance was measured using profit, profit margin, and sales. Like the classic Lieberson and O'Connor study (in this section), when taking into account control variables such as year, industry, and company, leadership appears to play a small role. However, if the analysis is based on the unexplained variance that remains after discounting the effects of the non-leadership variables, the study demonstrates that leadership differences do have a substantial impact.

The authors conclude by suggesting the statistics used in this and previous articles have been very simple. It would be useful to reanalyze the data using a within-organization design (thus holding constant industry and company variables).

Tosi, H. L., Jr., & Gomez-Mejia, L. R. (1994). CEO compensation monitoring and firm performance. *Academy of Management Journal, 37,* 1002-1016.

This study investigated the relationship between monitoring of CEO compensation and performance of the firm. Specifically it was hypothesized that (1) there is a curvilinear relationship between firm performance and the firm's monitoring of the CEO compensation process, and (2) that this relationship would be stronger in management-controlled firms than in owner-controlled firms. The curvilinear relationship was predicted such that a medium amount of monitoring would have the most positive impact on firm performance.

Hypotheses were tested using two separate studies. Study 1 involved chief compensation officers (CCOs) in 175 firms, and study 2 involved CCOs in 243 firms. In study 1 firm performance was measured using self-report indicators of levels of profitability, stock performance, and overall performance. In study 2 performance was measured using average earnings per share, average return on investment, average return on common stock, and average annual percent change in a firm's market value (all four were factor-analyzed into one factor).

CEO monitoring was measured using a self-report index describing the CEO pay-setting process and the policies and practices governing it. Firms with more than 5% of the company's stock owned by a single individual or institution were labeled owner-controlled. All of the other firms were labeled management-controlled. Both hypotheses were supported.

Zajac, E. J. (1990). CEO selection, succession, compensation and firm
     performance: A theoretical integration and empirical analysis. *Strategic
     Management Journal, 11,* 217-230.

     This study tested several hypotheses regarding CEOs and firm perfor-
mance (average return on assets during the CEO's tenure). Using surveys and
financial data on 105 firms from the Forbes or Fortune groups, results demonstrated that firms with insider CEOs tend to be significantly more profitable
than firms with outsider CEOs; firms whose CEOs have a specific successor
in mind tend to be significantly more profitable than firms whose CEOs do
not have a successor in mind; and firms whose CEOs perceive a stronger
connection between their personal financial wealth and the wealth of their
organization tend to be more profitable. There was no relationship between
CEO satisfaction and total compensation, nor was there a relationship between personal reputation and firm performance.

Attributable to Top Teams

Bantel, K. A., & Jackson, S. E. (1989). Top management and innovations in
     banking: Does the composition of the top team make a difference?
     Strategic Management Journal, 10, 107-124.

     This study examined the relationship between the demographic compo-
sition of top-management teams in the banking industry and innovation
(technical and administrative) using a sample of 199 banks. In this research,
innovation was defined as the number of innovative "items" (products,
programs, and services) firms had adopted or developed.
     Technical innovation included: products/services, marketing, comput-
erization, delivery systems and operations, and office automation. Administrative innovation included: staffing, attitude assessment, planning, compensation, and training. Demographic characteristics using the team as the unit of
analysis included: average age, average tenure in the firm, average education
level; and heterogeneity measures for age, tenure, educational background,
and functional background. Additionally, bank size, bank location, and team
size were controlled for. Results indicate that more innovative banks are
managed by more educated teams who are diverse with respect to their
functional area of expertise.

Eisenhardt, K. M., & Schoonhoven, C. B. (1990). Organizational growth: Linking founding team, strategy, environment, and growth among U.S. semiconductor ventures, 1978-1988. *Administrative Science Quarterly, 35,* 504-529.

This study explores the relationship between founding team demographics, technical strategy, and competitive environment with growth of new firms. Regarding founding team demographics, the authors hypothesized that greater previous joint work experience among the founding team, size of founding team, and greater variation in the industry experience of the founding team were all associated with higher growth among new firms.

Firm growth was measured as the difference in sales in each year of life through 1988 relative to sales at founding. Data were gathered from 92 semiconductor firms (from an original sample of 102 semiconductor firms that were single-business ventures founded exclusively to develop, produce, and sell semiconductor devices on the merchant market).

Hypotheses were supported using several analyses: regression using a four-year lag; even history analysis, successive regressions; and pooled cross-section regression. Interestingly, the effects of the founding team did not fade, but grew over time.

Finkelstein, S., & Hambrick, D. C. (1990). Top-management team tenure and organizational outcomes: The moderating role of managerial discretion. *Administrative Science Quarterly, 35,* 484-503.

This article proposed and tested the idea that discretion, or the latitude of action available to top executives, moderates the link between characteristics of the upper echelon and organizational outcomes. The authors looked at 100 organizations in three different industries: computer—high discretion; chemical—medium discretion; and natural gas—low discretion. They found that executive-team tenure had a significant effect on strategy and performance with longer-tenured teams that follow more persistent strategies, that conformed to industry standards, and exhibited average performance as compared to the industry.

Consistent with the theory, results differed depending on the level of managerial discretion between industries. Similarly, team tenure and organizational outcomes bore a stronger correspondence in small, high-discretion firms than in large, low-discretion firms.

Haleblian, J., & Finkelstein, S. (1993). Top-management team size, CEO
    dominance, and firm performance: The moderating roles of environ-
    mental turbulence and discretion. *Academy of Management Journal,
    36*(4), 844-863.

This study examined the effects of top-management team size (the
number of corporate officers who were also board members in each firm) and
CEO dominance (using a power index from ten objective measures of power
developed by Finkelstein [1992]) on firm performance (using return on assets,
return on sales, and return on equity) in different environments (turbulence
and discretion). The authors hypothesized that top-team size would be more
positively associated and CEO dominance would be more negatively associated with firm performance in a turbulent, high-discretion environment than
in a stable, low-discretion environment.

Data from forty-seven organizations in two industries (the computer
industry—turbulent and high discretion; and the natural gas distribution
industry—stable and low discretion) suggested that firms with large teams
performed better and firms with dominant CEOs performed worse in a
turbulent environment than in a stable one. In addition, the association between team size and CEO dominance with firm performance is significant in
a high-discretion environment but is not significant in a low-discretion
environment.

The study also controlled for firm size, strategic unrelatedness, efficiency, borrowing capacity, and tenure and functional heterogeneity. It should
be noted that turbulence and discretion were confounded as they were defined
by type of industry (the computer industry and the natural gas distribution
industry).

Hambrick, D. C., & D'Aveni, R. A. (1992). Top team deterioration as a part
    of the downward spiral of large corporate bankruptcies. *Management
    Review, 38*(10), 1445-1466.

In this exploratory study, the authors propose that the top-management
teams of failing firms differ from those in healthy firms, and that these
differences become more pronounced the closer the firms come to bank-

ruptcy. Data were collected on fifty-seven large bankruptcies and fifty-seven matched survivors using data for each of five years prior to the bankruptcy.

Results suggest that bankrupt firms demonstrated higher CEO dominance for up to five years prior to the failure. The top-management teams had shorter team tenure, and they tended to have extreme degrees of tenure similarity (either very homogeneous or very heterogeneous). Team compensation was lower, percentage of the team with core functional expertise was lower, and there was a tendency for smaller teams and fewer outside directors (but this was only significant for the year before bankruptcy). Using a limited test of causality, it appears that team deterioration is both a cause and an effect of performance deterioration.

Hambrick, D. C., & Mason, P. A. (1984). Upper echelons: The organization as a reflection of its top managers. *Academy of Management Review, 9*(2), 193-206.

This classic paper argues that top executives matter. Organizational outcomes—both strategies and effectiveness—are viewed as, in part, reflections of the values and cognitive bases of the top echelons in the organization. Using observable managerial characteristics (age, tenure, functional background, education, socioeconomic roots, and financial position), the authors develop a theory and propositions regarding how the characteristics of the top-management team affect outcomes both on average and using amount of dispersion (that is, heterogeneity).

Jackson, S. E. (1992). Consequences of group composition for the interpersonal dynamics of strategic issue processing. *Advances in Strategic Management, 8,* 345-382.

The object of this paper was to stimulate research to complement the work underway to test Hambrick and Mason's upper-echelons perspective (see Hambrick & Mason, 1984, in this section). To date, most upper-echelons research assumes that differences in team compositions translate into different team behaviors, which in turn translate into predictable organizational outcomes.

Jackson lays the groundwork for testing the intermediate processes, using strategic issue processing which includes creative decision making, problem solving, internal group processes such as conflict, and external liaison activities. In her review of the literature, the author finds that the links between the effects of group composition and outcomes are complex because the effects of composition vary across outcomes. The strategic-issue-processing perspective avoids these problems because strategic issues are examined separately. She concludes that for further development, typologies need to be developed for both group composition and strategic issue processing.

Murray, A. I. (1989). Top-management group heterogeneity and firm performance. *Strategic Management Journal, 10,* 125-141.

This study tests several hypotheses regarding the influence of top-team demographic heterogeneity on organizational performance, using a sample of eighty-four Fortune 500 companies in either the food or oil industries over a period of fourteen years (1967-1981). Organizational performance was measured in two ways. First, short-term efficiency performance was measured using ratios of earnings to sales, earnings to total capital, earnings to net worth, and earnings to equity. Second, for long-term "adaptability" performance, ratios of stock price to earnings and stock price to book value were used.

The results suggest a complex pattern of interrelationships depending on the industry studied, the lag between cause and effect, and type of performance measure. This suggests that the contribution of management to organizational performance is not constant.

Wiersema, M. F., & Bantel, K. A. (1992). Top management team demography and corporate strategic change. *Academy of Management Journal, 35,* 91-121.

In this study, the relationship between the demography of top-management teams and corporate strategic change was examined. The authors argued that demographic characteristics (using both central tendency variables and dispersion variables) reflect top managers' cognitive perspectives. Corporate strategy was defined as decisions on the mix and emphases of business within a portfolio, including the evaluation of appropriate courses of action with regard to potential divestments, downsizings, and of existing businesses; as well as to acquisitions, mergers, and the development of new businesses. Change was measured by the absolute percentage change in diversification strategy over the period 1980 to 1983, using Jacquemin and Berry's entropy measure of diversification [Jacquemin, A. P., & Berry, C. H. (1979). Entropy measures of diversification and corporate growth. *Journal of Industrial Economics, 27,* 359-369].

Using 87 firms (out of 100 firms randomly sampled from the 500 largest manufacturing firms for the year 1980—as listed in *Fortune*), and controlling for prior firm performance, organizational size, top-team size, and industry structure, the authors found that firms that underwent changes in corporate strategy were characterized by top-management teams with lower average age, shorter organizational tenure, higher team tenure, higher educational level, higher educational specialization heterogeneity, and higher academic training in the sciences.

Author Index

CENTER FOR CREATIVE LEADERSHIP PUBLICATIONS

SELECTED REPORTS:

The Adventures of Team Fantastic: A Practical Guide for Team Leaders and Members
G.L. Hallam (1996, Stock #172) $20.00

CEO Selection: A Street-smart Review G.P. Hollenbeck (1994, Stock #164) $25.00

Choosing 360: A Guide to Evaluating Multi-rater Feedback Instruments for Management
Development E. Van Velsor, J. Brittain Leslie, & J.W. Fleenor (1997, Stock #334) $15.00

Creativity in the R&D Laboratory T.M. Amabile & S.S. Gryskiewicz (1987, Stock #130) $12.00

A Cross-National Comparison of Effective Leadership and Teamwork: Toward a Global
Workforce J.B. Leslie & E. Van Velsor (1998, Stock #177) $15.00

Eighty-eight Assignments for Development in Place: Enhancing the Developmental Challenge
of Existing Jobs M.M. Lombardo & R.W. Eichinger (1989, Stock #136) $15.00

Enhancing 360-degree Feedback for Senior Executives: How to Maximize the Benefits and
Minimize the Risks R.E. Kaplan & C.J. Palus (1994, Stock #160) $15.00

Evolving Leaders: A Model for Promoting Leadership Development in Programs C.J. Palus &
W.H. Drath (1995, Stock #165) $15.00

Forceful Leadership and Enabling Leadership: You Can Do Both R.E. Kaplan (1996, Stock #171) $15.00

Formal Mentoring Programs in Organizations: An Annotated Bibliography C.A. Douglas
(1997, Stock #332) $20.00

Four Essential Ways that Coaching Can Help Executives R. Witherspoon & R.P. White (1997,
Stock #175) $10.00

Gender Differences in the Development of Managers: How Women Managers Learn From
Experience E. Van Velsor & M. W. Hughes (1990, Stock #145) $35.00

A Glass Ceiling Survey: Benchmarking Barriers and Practices A.M. Morrison, C.T. Schreiber,
& K.F. Price (1995, Stock #161) $15.00

Helping Leaders Take Effective Action: A Program Evaluation D.P. Young & N.M. Dixon
(1996, Stock #174) $18.00

How to Design an Effective System for Developing Managers and Executives M.A. Dalton &
G.P. Hollenbeck (1996, Stock #158) $15.00

Inside View: A Leader's Observations on Leadership W.F. Ulmer, Jr. (1997, Stock #176) $12.00

The Intuitive Pragmatists: Conversations with Chief Executive Officers J.S. Bruce (1986,
Stock #310) $12.00

Leadership for Turbulent Times L.R. Sayles (1995, Stock #325) $15.00

A Look at Derailment Today: North America and Europe J. Brittain Leslie & E. Van Velsor
(1996, Stock #169) $20.00

Making Common Sense: Leadership as Meaning-making in a Community of Practice
W.H. Drath & C.J. Palus (1994, Stock #156) $15.00

Managerial Promotion: The Dynamics for Men and Women M.N. Ruderman, P.J. Ohlott, &
K.E. Kram (1996, Stock #170) $15.00

Managing Across Cultures: A Learning Framework M.S. Wilson, M.H. Hoppe, & L.R. Sayles
(1996, Stock #173) $15.00

Perspectives on Dialogue: Making Talk Developmental for Individuals and Organizations
N.M. Dixon (1996, Stock #168) $20.00

Preventing Derailment: What To Do Before It's Too Late M.M. Lombardo & R.W. Eichinger
(1989, Stock #138) $25.00

The Realities of Management Promotion M.N. Ruderman & P.J. Ohlott (1994, Stock #157) $15.00

Selection at the Top: An Annotated Bibliography V.I. Sessa & R.J. Campbell (1997, Stock #333)... $20.00

Should 360-degree Feedback Be Used Only for Developmental Purposes? D.W. Bracken,
M.A. Dalton, R.A. Jako, C.D. McCauley, V.A. Pollman, with Preface by G.P. Hollenbeck (1997,
Stock #335) $15.00

Succession Planning: An Annotated Bibliography L.J. Eastman (1995, Stock #324) $20.00

Training for Action: A New Approach to Executive Development R.M. Burnside &
V.A. Guthrie (1992, Stock #153) $15.00

Twenty-two Ways to Develop Leadership in Staff Managers R.W. Eichinger & M.M. Lombardo
(1990, Stock #144) $15.00

Using 360-degree Feedback in Organizations: An Annotated Bibliography J.W. Fleenor & J.M. Prince (1997, Stock #338) $15.00
Using an Art Technique to Facilitate Leadership Development C. De Ciantis (1995, Stock #166) ... $15.00
Why Managers Have Trouble Empowering: A Theoretical Perspective Based on Concepts of Adult Development W.H. Drath (1993, Stock #155) $15.00

SELECTED BOOKS:
Balancing Act: How Managers Can Integrate Successful Careers and Fulfilling Personal Lives J.R. Kofodimos (1993, Stock #247) $28.00
Beyond Ambition: How Driven Managers Can Lead Better and Live Better R.E. Kaplan, W.H. Drath, & J.R. Kofodimos (1991, Stock #227) $32.95
Breaking Free: A Prescription for Personal and Organizational Change D.M. Noer (1997, Stock #271) $25.00
Breaking the Glass Ceiling: Can Women Reach the Top of America's Largest Corporations? (Updated Edition) A.M. Morrison, R.P. White, & E. Van Velsor (1992, Stock #236A) $13.00
Choosing to Lead (Second Edition) K.E. Clark & M.B. Clark (1996, Stock #327) $25.00
Discovering Creativity: Proceedings of the 1992 International Creativity and Innovation Networking Conference S.S. Gryskiewicz (Ed.) (1993, Stock #319) $30.00
Executive Selection: A Look at What We Know and What We Need to Know D.L. DeVries (1993, Stock #321) $20.00
Healing the Wounds: Overcoming the Trauma of Layoffs and Revitalizing Downsized Organizations D.M. Noer (1993, Stock #245) $29.50
High Flyers: Developing the Next Generation of Leaders M.W. McCall, Jr. (1997, Stock #293) $27.95
If I'm In Charge Here, Why Is Everybody Laughing? D.P. Campbell (1984, Stock #205) $9.95
If You Don't Know Where You're Going You'll Probably End Up Somewhere Else D.P. Campbell (1974, Stock #203) $9.95
Inklings: Collected Columns on Leadership and Creativity D.P. Campbell (1992, Stock #233) $15.00
Leadership: Enhancing the Lessons of Experience (Second Edition) R.L. Hughes, R.C. Ginnett, & G.J. Curphy (1996, Stock #266) $55.00
The Lessons of Experience: How Successful Executives Develop on the Job M.W. McCall, Jr., M.M. Lombardo, & A.M. Morrison (1988, Stock #211) $24.95
Making Diversity Happen: Controversies and Solutions A.M. Morrison, M.N. Ruderman, & M. Hughes-James (1993, Stock #320) $20.00
The New Leaders: Guidelines on Leadership Diversity in America A.M. Morrison (1992, Stock #238) $32.00
Readings in Innovation S.S. Gryskiewicz & D.A. Hills (Eds.) (1992, Stock #240) $25.00
Selected Research on Work Team Diversity M.N. Ruderman, M.W. Hughes-James, & S.E. Jackson (Eds.) (1996, Stock #326) $24.95
Staying on Track L.D. Coble & D.L. Brubaker (1997, Stock #280) $18.95
Take the Road to Creativity and Get Off Your Dead End D.P. Campbell (1977, Stock #204) $9.95
The Working Leader: The Triumph of High Performance Over Conventional Management Principles L.R. Sayles (1993, Stock #243) $20.00

SPECIAL PACKAGES:
Development and Derailment (Stock #702; includes 136, 138, & 144) $35.00
The Diversity Collection (Stock #708; includes 145, 177, 236A, 238, 317, & 320) $85.00
Executive Selection (Stock #710; includes 141, 321, 333, & 157) $50.00
Gender Research (Stock #716; includes 145, 161, 170, 236A, & 238) $90.00
HR Professional's Info Pack (Stock #717; includes 136, 158, 165, 169, 324, & 334) $75.00
New Understanding of Leadership (Stock #718; includes 156, 165, & 168) $40.00
Personal Growth, Taking Charge, and Enhancing Creativity (Stock #231; includes 203, 204, & 205) $20.00

Discounts are available. Please write for a comprehensive Publications catalog. Address your request to: Publication, Center for Creative Leadership, P.O. Box 26300, Greensboro, NC 27438-6300, 336-545-2805, or fax to 336-545-3221. All prices subject to change.

ORDER FORM

Or E-mail your order via the Center's online bookstore at www.ccl.org

Name _____ Title _____

Organization _____

Mailing Address _____
(street address required for mailing)

City/State/Zip _____

Telephone _____ FAX _____
(telephone number required for UPS mailing)

Quantity	Stock No.	Title	Unit Cost	Amount

CCL's Federal ID Number is 237-07-9591.

Subtotal	
Shipping and Handling (add 6% of subtotal with a $4.00 minimum; add 40% on all international shipping)	
NC residents add 6% sales tax; CA residents add 7.75% sales tax; CO residents add 6.2% sales tax	
TOTAL	

METHOD OF PAYMENT
(ALL orders for less than $100 must be PREPAID.)

❏ Check or money order enclosed (payable to Center for Creative Leadership).

❏ Purchase Order No. _____ (Must be accompanied by this form.)

❏ Charge my order, plus shipping, to my credit card:
   ❏ American Express   ❏ Discover   ❏ MasterCard   ❏ VISA

ACCOUNT NUMBER:_____ EXPIRATION DATE: MO.____ YR.____

NAME OF ISSUING BANK: _____

SIGNATURE _____

❏ Please put me on your mailing list.

Publication • Center for Creative Leadership • P.O. Box 26300
Greensboro, NC 27438-6300
336-545-2805 • FAX 336-545-3221

Client Priority Code: R

fold here

CENTER FOR CREATIVE LEADERSHIP
PUBLICATION
P.O. Box 26300
Greensboro, NC 27438-6300